Learning the UNIX
Operating System
Fourth Edition

Jerry Peek, Grace Todino, and John Strang

O'REILLY™

Cambridge · Köln · Paris · Sebastopol · Tokyo

Learning the UNIX Operating System, 4th Edition

by Jerry Peek, Grace Todino, and John Strang

Copyright © 1998, 1993, 1987, 1986 O'Reilly & Associates, Inc. All rights reserved.
Printed in the United States of America.

Editor: Tim O'Reilly

Update Editor: Gigi Estabrook

Production Editor: Nancy Wolfe Kotary

Printing History:

1986:	First Edition. Written by Grace Todino and John Strang.
1987:	Second Edition. Revised by Tim O'Reilly.
April 1989:	Minor corrections.
August 1993:	Third Edition. Additions and revisions by Jerry Peek.
June 1994:	Minor corrections.
January 1998:	Fourth Edition. Additions and revisions by Jerry Peek.

This book is printed on acid-free paper with 85% recycled content, 15% post-consumer waste. O'Reilly & Associates is committed to using paper with the highest recycled content available consistent with high quality.

ISBN: 1-56592-390-1   [8/98]

Learning the UNIX Operating System

Table of Contents

Preface

The UNIX Operating System

An *operating system* (or "OS") is a set of programs that controls a computer. It controls both the *hardware* (things you can touch—such as keyboards, displays, and disk drives) and the *software* (application programs that you run, such as a word processor).

Some computers have a *single-user* OS, which means only one person can use the computer at a time. Many older OSes (like DOS) can also do only one job at a time. But almost any computer can do a lot more if it has a *multiuser, multitasking* operating system like UNIX. These powerful OSes let many people use the computer at the same time and let each user run several jobs at once.

UNIX was invented almost 30 years ago for scientific and professional users who wanted a very powerful and flexible OS. It's been significantly developed since then. Because UNIX was designed for experts, it can be a bit overwhelming at first. But after you get the basics (from this book!) you'll start to appreciate some of the reasons to use UNIX:

- It comes with a huge number of powerful application programs. You can get many others for free on the Internet. (The GNU utilities, freely available from the Free Software Foundation, are very popular.) You can thus do much more at a much lower cost.

- Not only are the applications often free, but some versions of UNIX itself are also free. Linux is a good example. Like the free applications, these free versions of UNIX are usually of excellent quality. They're maintained by volunteer programmers who want a powerful OS and are frustrated by the slow, bug-ridden development of OSes at big companies.

- Much of the development of the Internet was done on UNIX systems. Many Internet web sites and Internet service providers use UNIX because it's so powerful, flexible, and inexpensive.

- UNIX runs on almost any kind of hardware. After you learn UNIX on one system, you'll know how to use it on any other system.

Versions of UNIX

There are many different versions of UNIX. Until a few years ago, there were two main versions: the line of UNIX releases that started at AT&T (the latest is System V Release 4), and another line from the University of California at Berkeley (the latest version is BSD 4.4). Some other major commercial versions include SunOS, Solaris, SCO UNIX, AIX, HP/UX, and ULTRIX. The freely available versions include Linux and FreeBSD.

Many versions of UNIX, including System V Release 4, merge earlier AT&T releases with BSD features. The recent POSIX standard for UNIX-like operating systems defines a single interface to UNIX. Although advanced features differ among systems, you should be able to use this introductory handbook on any type of system.

UNIX can be used the way it was originally designed, on typewriter-like terminals. Most versions of UNIX can also work with window systems, which allow each user to have more than one "terminal" on a single display. Chapter 2, *Using Window Systems*, shows the basics of a window system. All other chapters are for every UNIX user—with or without a window system.

What This Handbook Covers

Learning the UNIX Operating System teaches the basic system utility commands to get you started with UNIX. Instead of overwhelming you with a lot of details, we want you to be comfortable in the UNIX environment as soon as possible. So we cover the most useful features of a command instead of describing all its options in detail. Appendix A, *Reading List*, lists other references.

After reading this handbook, you should be able to:

- Log in and log out of your system

- Control the system with control characters

- Send messages to other users

- Manage UNIX files and directories, including listing, creating, copying, printing, and removing files, and moving in and out of directories

- Work more efficiently using UNIX pipes, filters, and multitasking

What's New in the Fourth Edition

UNIX keeps evolving; this book changes with it. Although most of the tips in this book work on all UNIX systems—old and new—there have been changes since 1993 that justify a fourth edition. A major change is the emergence of Linux as a very popular version of UNIX. Linux has some unique features that even beginners will appreciate. We've also made changes suggested by our readers.

Format

The following sections describe the conventions used in this handbook.

Commands

We introduce each main concept, then break it down into task-oriented sections. Each section shows the best command to use for a task, explains what it does, and the syntax (the way to put the command line together). The syntax is given like this:

> **rm** *filename*

Commands appear in **boldface** type (in this example, **rm**). You should type the command exactly as it appears in the example. The variable parts (here, *filename*) will appear in *italic* type; you must supply your own value. To enter this command, you would type **rm** followed by a space and the name of the file that you want to remove, then press the RETURN key. (Your keyboard may have a key labeled ENTER, or an arrow with a right-angle shaft, instead of a RETURN key.) Throughout this book, the term *enter* means to type a command and press RETURN to run it.

Examples

Examples show what should happen as you enter a command. Some examples assume that you've created certain files. If you haven't, you may not get the results shown.

We use typewriter-style characters for examples. Items you type to try the example are **boldface**. System messages and responses are `normal text`.

Here's an example:

```
% date
Tue Nov  4 13:39:24 EST 1997
%
```

The character "%" is the shell (system) prompt. To do this example, you would type **date** and then press RETURN. The **date** command responds "Tue Nov 4 13:39:24 EST 1997" and then returns you to the prompt.

Problem Checklist

We've included a problem checklist in some sections. You may skip these parts and go back to them if you have a problem.

Exercises

Many sections have exercises to reinforce the text you've read. Follow the exercises, but don't be afraid to experiment on your own.

The exercises have two columns: the left-hand column tells you what to do and the right-hand column tells you how to do it. For example, a line in the exercise near the end of Chapter 1, *Getting Started*, shows:

   Get today's date   Enter **date**

To follow the exercise, you type in the word **date** on your keyboard and then press the RETURN key. The left-hand column tells you what will happen.

After you try the commands, you'll have a better idea of the ones you want to learn more about. You can then look them up in your system's UNIX documentation or use one of the other references listed in Appendix A.

A Note to Our Readers

We update each book periodically. This allows us to incorporate changes suggested to us by our readers. We'd like new users to benefit from your experience as well as ours.

If you have a suggestion, or solve a significant problem that our handbook does not cover, please write to or call us at the following address and let us know about it (include information about your UNIX environment and the computer you use):

O'Reilly & Associates, Inc.
101 Morris Street
Sebastopol, CA 95472
1-800-998-9938 (in US or Canada)
1-707-829-0515 (international/local)
1-707-829-0104 (FAX)

If you have access to electronic mail (Chapter 3, *Your UNIX Account*), you may email your comments to:

bookquestions@oreilly.com

You'll have our thanks, along with thanks from future readers of this handbook.

Acknowledgments

Parts of Chapter 2, *Using Window Systems*, were adapted from O'Reilly & Associates' *X Window System User's Guide, Volume 3, OSF/Motif Edition*, by Valerie Quercia and Tim O'Reilly. Valerie Quercia reviewed the revised Chapter 2.

Gigi Estabrook was the update editor for the fourth edition, and Nancy Wolfe Kotary was the production editor and copyedited the new edition. Madeleine Newell proofread the fourth edition; Seth Maislin wrote the index; Sheryl Avruch, Nicole Gipson Arigo, and Mary Anne Mayo provided quality control checks; and Elissa Haney provided production assistance.

1

Getting Started

Working in the UNIX Environment

Before you can start using UNIX, your system administrator has to set up a UNIX account for you. Think of this account as your office—it's your place in the UNIX environment. Other users may also be at work on the same system. At many sites, there will be a whole network of UNIX computers. So in addition to knowing your account name, you may also need to know the *hostname* (name) of the computer that has your account.

Each user communicates with the computer from a terminal or a window. To get into the UNIX environment, you first connect to the UNIX computer. (You may have a terminal that's already connected to the computer.) Next, you start a session by logging in to your UNIX account. Logging in does two things: it identifies which user is in a session, and it tells the computer that you're ready to start working. When you've finished working, you log out—and, if necessary, disconnect from the UNIX computer.

Connecting to the UNIX Computer

If you turn on your terminal and see a message from the UNIX computer that looks something like this:

```
login:
```

you can probably skip ahead to the section "Logging In" later in this chapter. Otherwise, browse through the next few sections and find the one that applies to you. (We can't cover every user's situation exactly. If none of these suggestions helps you enough, ask another UNIX user or your system administrator.)

Connecting from another operating system

If you're using a personal computer to connect to the UNIX system, you'll probably need to start a *terminal emulation* program. Some common programs are **procomm**, **qmodem**, **kermit**, **minicom**, and **telnet**. (There are lots of others.)

If you start the program and get a UNIX "login:" prompt, you're ready to log in. But if your screen stays blank or you get another message that you don't understand, check with another user or your system administrator for help.

Connecting with a data switch

Your office may have a data switch, a port contender, or another system that allows you to select which computer you will connect to. Like a telephone switchboard, this connects your terminal to one of a number of computers. Enter your computer's hostname or code number at the prompt—or choose from the menu of hosts.

Connecting from a window system

If you have an X terminal or a workstation, you should read the introductory sections of Chapter 2, *Using Window Systems* to help you find the right steps for logging in.

Logging In

The process of making yourself known to the UNIX computer system and getting to your UNIX account is called *logging in*. Before you can start work, you must connect your terminal or window to the UNIX computer (see the previous sections). Then log in to UNIX and identify yourself. To log in, enter your username (usually your name or initials) and a private password. The password does not appear on the screen as you enter it.

When you log in successfully, you will get some system messages and finally the UNIX shell prompt (where you can enter UNIX commands). A successful login to the system named *nutshell* would look something like this:

```
O'Reilly & Associates, Inc.
nutshell.oreilly.com: Solaris UNIX version 2.5
```

```
login: john
Password:
Last login: Mon Nov  3 14:34:51 EST 1997 from joe_pc

------------- NOTICE TO ALL USERS ----------------
The hosts nutshell, mongo and cruncher will be down
for maintenance from 6 to 9 PM tonight.
--------------------------------------------------

My opinions may have changed, but not the fact that I am right.
Tue Nov  4 12:24:48 EST 1997
%
```

In this example, the system messages include a "fortune" and the date. Although this example doesn't show it, you may be asked for your *terminal type*, accounting or chargeback information, and so on. The last line to appear is the UNIX shell prompt. When you reach this point, you're logged in to your account and can start using UNIX commands.

Instead of a shell prompt, you may get a menu of choices ("email," "news," and so on). If one of the choices is something like "shell prompt" or "command prompt," select it. Then you'll be able to follow the descriptions and examples in this book.

The messages that appear when you log in differ from system to system and day to day. The shell prompt also differs. The examples in this book use the percentage sign as a prompt (%).

Let's summarize logging in, step by step:

1. If needed, connect your terminal or window to the UNIX system.

2. If you don't have a "login:" prompt, press the RETURN key a few times until you see that prompt on the screen.

3. Type in your username in *lowercase letters* at the prompt. For example, if your login name is "john," type:

   ```
   login: john
   ```

   Press the RETURN key.

   The system should prompt you to enter your password. If passwords aren't used on your system, you can skip the next step.

4. If you were assigned a password, type it at the prompt. For security, your password is not displayed as you type it:

   ```
   Password:
   ```

   Press the RETURN key after you finish typing your password.

The system verifies your account name and password, and, if they're correct, logs you in to your account.

Problem checklist

Nothing seemed to happen after I logged in.

> Wait a minute, since the system may just be slow. If you still don't get anything, ask other users if they're having the same problem.

The system says "login incorrect".

> Try logging in again, taking care to enter the correct name and password. Be sure to type your username at the "login:" prompt and your password at the "password:" prompt. Backspacing may not work while entering either of these; if you make a mistake, use RETURN to get a new "login:" prompt and try again. Also make sure to use the exact combination of upper- and lowercase letters your password contains.

> If you still fail after trying to log in a few more times, check with your system administrator to make sure you're using the right username and password for your account.

All letters are in UPPERCASE and/or have backslashes (\\) before them.

> You probably entered your username in uppercase letters. Type **exit** and log in again.

Remote Logins

The computer you log in to may not be the computer you need to use. For instance, you might have a workstation on your desk but need to do some work on the main computer in another building. Or you might be a professor doing research with a computer at another university.

Your UNIX system can probably connect to another computer to let you work as if you were sitting at the other computer. To do this, you first log in to your local computer. Then you start a program on your local computer that connects to the remote computer. Some typical programs are **telnet** and **rlogin** (for connecting over a computer network) as well as **cu** and **tip** (for connecting through telephone lines using a modem). You use the remote system until you're done; when you log off the remote computer, the remote-login program quits, and then returns you to your local computer.

The syntax for most remote-login programs is:

> *program-name remote-hostname*

For example, if Dr. Nelson wanted to connect to the remote computer named *biolab.medu.edu*, she'd log in to her local computer (named *fuzzy*) first. Next, she'd use the **telnet** program to reach the remote computer. Her session might look something like this:

```
login: jennifer
Password:

NOTICE to all second-floor MDs: meeting in room 304 at 4 PM.

fuzzy% telnet biolab.medu.edu
Medical University Biology Laboratory

biolab.medu.edu login: jdnelson
Password:

biolab%
          .

          .

          .
biolab% exit
Connection closed by foreign host.
fuzzy%
```

Her accounts have shell prompts that include the hostname. This reminds her when she's logged in remotely. If you use more than one system but don't have the hostname in your prompt, references in Appendix A, *Reading List* (*UNIX Power Tools*, for example), will show you how to add it.

The UNIX Shell

Once you've logged in, you're working with a program called a *shell*. The shell interprets the commands you enter, runs the program you've asked for, and generally coordinates what happens between you and the UNIX operating system. Common shells include Bourne (**sh**), Korn (**ksh**), and C (**csh**) shells, as well as **bash** and **tcsh**.

For a beginner, the differences between most shells are slight. If you plan to do a lot of work with UNIX, though, ask your system administrator which shell your account uses; you should learn more about your shell and its set of special commands.

The Shell Prompt

When the system finishes running a command, the shell replies with a prompt to tell you that you can enter another command line.

Shell prompts usually contain $ or %. The prompt can be customized, though, so your own shell prompt may be different.

Entering a Command Line

Entering a command line at the shell prompt tells the computer what to do. Each command line includes the name of a UNIX program. When you press RETURN, the shell interprets your command line and executes the program.

The first word that you type at a shell prompt is always a UNIX command (program name). Like most things in UNIX, command names are case-sensitive; if the command name is lowercase (and most are), you must type it in lowercase. Some simple command lines have just one word: the command name.

date

An example single-word command line is **date**. Entering the command **date** displays the current date and time:

```
% date
Tue Nov  4 13:39:24 EST 1997
%
```

As you type a command line, the system simply collects your input from the keyboard. Pressing the RETURN key tells the shell that you have finished entering text and that it can start executing the command.

who

Another simple command is **who**. It lists each logged-on user's username, terminal number, and login time.

The **who** command can also tell you who is logged in at the terminal you're using. The command line is **who am i**. This command line consists of the command (**who**) and arguments (**am i**). (The section "Syntax of UNIX Command Lines," later in this chapter, explains arguments.)

```
% who am i
cactus!john     tty23   Nov  6 08:26      (rose)
```

The response shown in this example says that:

- "I am" John.

- I'm logged on to the computer named "cactus."

- I'm using terminal 23.

- I logged in at 8:26 on the morning of November 6.

- I started my login from another computer named "rose."

Not all versions of **who am i** give the same information.

Correcting a Mistake

What if you make a mistake in a command line? Suppose you typed **dare** instead of **date** and pressed the RETURN key before you realized your mistake. The shell will give you an error message:

```
% dare
dare: command not found
%
```

Don't be too concerned about getting error messages. Sometimes you'll get an error even if it appears that you typed the command correctly. This can be caused by typing control characters that are invisible on the screen. Once the prompt returns, reenter your command.

Most modern shells let you recall previous commands and edit command lines. If you'll be doing a lot of work at the shell prompt, it's worth learning these handy techniques. They take more time to learn than we can spend here, though. Ask other users for help or read a reference book for your shell (see Appendix A). We'll concentrate on simple methods that work with all shells.

If you see a mistake before you press RETURN, you can use the BACKSPACE key to erase the mistake and put in the correction.

The *erase character* differs from system to system and from account to account, and can be customized. The most common erase characters are:

- BACKSPACE

- DELETE, DEL, or RUBOUT key

- CTRL-H

CTRL-H is called a *control character*. To type a control character (for example, CTRL-H), hold down the CTRL key while pressing the letter "h". (This is like the way you make an uppercase letter: hold the SHIFT key while pressing a letter key.) In the text, we will write control characters as CTRL-H, but in the examples, we will use the standard notation: ^H. This is *not* the same as pressing the ^ (caret) key, letting go, and then typing an H!

The key labeled DEL may be used as the *interrupt character* instead of the erase character. (It's labeled DELETE or RUBOUT on some terminals.) This key is used to interrupt or cancel a command, and can be used in many (but not all) cases when you want to quit what you're doing. Another character often programmed to do the same thing is CTRL-C.

Some other common control characters are:

CTRL-U

    Erases the whole input line; you can start over.

CTRL-S

    Pauses output from a program that is writing to the screen.

CTRL-Q

    Restarts output after a pause by CTRL-S.

CTRL-D

    Used to signal end-of-input for some programs (like **cat** and **mail**; see Chapter 3, *Your UNIX Account*) and return you to a shell prompt. If you type CTRL-D at a shell prompt, it may also log you out of the UNIX system.

Find the erase and interrupt characters for your account and write them down:

    _____   Backspace and erase a character

    _____   Interrupt a command

In Chapter 3, we'll tell you how to change these characters if you like.

Logging Out

To end a UNIX session, you must log out. You should *not* end a session by just turning off your terminal! To log out, enter the command **exit**. (In many cases, the command **logout** will also work.) Depending on your shell, you may also be able to log out by typing CTRL-D.

What happens next depends on the place from which you've logged in:

- If your terminal is connected directly to the computer, the "login:" prompt should appear on the screen.

- If you're using a window system, the window will probably close. If you have additional windows open, you'll need to log out or close them, too. You may also need to terminate the window system itself. (See Chapter 2.)

- If you were connected to a remote computer, the system prompt from your local computer should reappear on your screen. (That is, you're still logged in to your local computer.) Repeat the process if you want to log out from the local computer.

After you've logged out, you can turn off your terminal or leave it on for the next user.

Problem checklist

The first few times you use UNIX, you aren't likely to have any of the following problems. However, you may have these problems later, as you start doing more advanced work.

You get another shell prompt or the system says "logout: not login shell."
  You've been using a subshell (a shell created by your original login shell). To end each subshell, type **exit** (or just type [CTRL-D]) until you're logged out.

The system says "There are stopped jobs."
  Many UNIX systems have a feature called *job control* that lets you suspend a program temporarily while it's running. One or more of the programs you ran during your session has not ended, but is stopped (paused). Enter **fg** to bring each stopped job into the foreground, then quit the program normally. (See Chapter 6, *Multitasking.*)

Syntax of UNIX Command Lines

UNIX command lines can be simple, one-word entries like the **date** command. They can also be more complex: you may need to type more than the command name.

A UNIX command may or may not have *arguments*. An argument can be an option or a filename. The general format for UNIX commands is:

  command *option(s) filename(s)*

There isn't a single set of rules for writing UNIX commands and arguments, but you can use these general rules in most cases:

- Enter commands in lowercase.

- *Options* modify the way in which a command works. Options are often single letters prefixed with a dash (–) and set off by any number of spaces or tabs. Multiple options in one command line can be set off individually (like **–a –b**), or, in some cases, you can combine them after a single dash (like **–ab**).

Some commands, including those on Linux systems, also have options made from complete words or phrases, like **−−delete** or **−−confirm-delete**. When you enter a command, you can use this option style, the single-letter options (which all start with a single dash), or both.

- The argument *filename* is the name of a file that you want to use. If you don't enter a filename correctly, you may get the response "*filename*: no such file or directory" or "*filename*: cannot open."

  Some commands, like **telnet** and **who** (shown earlier in this chapter), have arguments that aren't filenames.

- You must type spaces between commands, options, and filenames.

- Options come before filenames.

- Two or more commands can be written on the same command line, each separated by a semicolon (;). Commands entered this way are executed one after another by the shell.

UNIX has a lot of commands! Don't try to memorize all of them. In fact, you'll probably need to know just a few commands and their options. As time goes on, you'll learn these commands and the best way to use them for your job. We cover some useful UNIX commands in later chapters.

Let's look at a sample UNIX command. The **ls** command displays a list of files. It can be used with or without options and arguments. If you enter:

```
% ls
```

a list of filenames will be displayed on the screen. But if you enter:

```
% ls -l
```

there will be an entire line of information for each file. The **−l** option (a dash and a lowercase letter "l") modifies the normal output of the **ls** command and lists files in the long format. You can also get information about a particular file by using its name as the second argument. For example, to find out about a file called *chap1*, enter:

```
% ls -l chap1
```

Many UNIX commands have more than one option. For instance, **ls** has the **−a** (*all*) option for listing hidden files. You can use multiple options in either of these ways:

```
% ls -a -l
% ls -al
```

You must type one space between the command name and the dash that introduces the options. If you enter **ls–al**, the shell will say "ls-al: command not found."

Exercise: Entering a few commands

The best way to get used to UNIX is to enter some commands. To run a command, type in the command and then press the [RETURN] key. Remember that almost all UNIX commands are typed in lowercase.

Get today's date.	Enter **date**
List logged-in users.	Enter **who**
Obtain more information about users.	Enter **who -u** or **finger** or **w**
Find out who is at your terminal.	Enter **who am i**
Enter two commands in the same line.	Enter **who am i;date**
Mistype a command.	Enter **woh**

In this session, you've tried several simple commands and seen the results on the screen.

Types of Commands

The previous section was about UNIX commands you enter at a shell prompt. Some UNIX commands have commands of their own. (For examples, look at the **more**, **mail**, and **pg** commands in Chapter 3. Text editors like **vi** and **emacs** also have their own commands.) Once you start the command, it prints its own prompt and understands its own set of commands (not UNIX commands).

For instance, if you enter **mail**, you'll see a new prompt from the **mail** program. You'll enter mail commands to handle mail messages. When you enter the special command (q) to quit the **mail** program, **mail** will stop prompting you. Then you'll get another shell prompt; you can enter UNIX commands again.

The Unresponsive Terminal

During your UNIX session (while you're logged in), your terminal may not respond when you type a command, or the display on your screen may stop at an unusual place. That's called a "hung" or "frozen" terminal or session.

A session can be hung for several reasons. One of the most common is that the connection between your terminal and the computer gets too busy and your terminal has to wait its turn. (Other users or computers are probably sharing the same connection.) In that case, your session will start by itself in a few moments. You should *not* try to "un-hang" the session by entering extra commands because those commands will all take effect after the connection resumes.

If the system doesn't respond for quite a while (and how long that is depends on your individual situation; ask your system administrator for advice), the following solutions will usually work. Try these in the order shown until the system responds.

1. Press the RETURN key.

   You may have typed a command but forgotten to press RETURN to tell the shell that you're done typing and it should now interpret the command.

2. If you can type commands, but nothing happens when you press RETURN, try pressing LINE FEED or typing CTRL-J. If this works, your terminal needs to be reset to fix the RETURN key. Some systems have a **reset** command that you can run by typing CTRL-J **reset** CTRL-J. If this doesn't work, you may need to log out and log back in or turn your terminal off and on again.

3. If your shell has job control (see Chapter 6), type CTRL-Z.

   This suspends a program that may be running and gives you another shell prompt. Now you can enter the **jobs** command to find the program's name, then restart the program with **fg** or terminate it with **kill**.

4. Use your interrupt key (found earlier in this chapter—typically DELETE or CTRL-C).

   This interrupts a program that may be running. (Unless a program is run in the background, as described in Chapter 6, the shell will wait for it to finish before giving a new prompt. A long-running program may thus appear to hang the terminal.) If this doesn't work the first time, try it once more; doing it more than twice usually won't help.

5. Type CTRL-Q.

   If output has been stopped with CTRL-S, this will restart it. (Note that some systems will automatically issue CTRL-S if they need to pause output; this character may not have been typed from the keyboard.)

6. Check that the NO SCROLL key is not locked or toggled on.

   This key stops the screen display from scrolling upward. If your keyboard has a NO SCROLL key that can be toggled on and off by pressing it over and over, keep track of how many times you've pressed it as you try to free yourself. If it doesn't seem to help, be sure you've pressed it an even number of times; this leaves the key in the same state it was when you started.

7. Check the physical connection from the terminal to the system.

8. Type CTRL-D at the beginning of a new line.

   Some programs (like **mail**) expect text from the user. A program may be waiting for an end-of-input character from you to tell it that you've finished entering text. Typing CTRL-D may cause you to log out, so you should try this only as a last resort.

9. If you're using a window system, close (terminate) the window you're using and open a new one. Otherwise, turn your terminal off, wait ten seconds or so, then turn it on again (this may also log you out).

If none of these works, you should then ask a local system expert for help and watch carefully.

2

Using Window Systems

Introduction to Windowing

All versions of UNIX work with computer terminals that handle a single window or a single login session. Most modern UNIX versions support one or more *window systems*. A window system is a package of programs that let a terminal handle many sessions at once. Along with the keyboard, window systems use a *mouse* or another device (such as a trackball) to move a *pointer* across the screen. The pointer can select parts of the screen, move them, help you copy and paste text, work with menus of commands, and more. If you've used a Macintosh, any version of Microsoft Windows, or OS/2 and its Presentation Manager (among others), you've used a window system. Figure 2-1 shows a typical display with windows.

Here's a special note for Linux users. Most Linux systems support window systems. But they also have a surprisingly handy substitute: *virtual consoles*. If you're using the terminal that's directly connected to a personal computer running Linux, you can access up to eight separate screens on the same display. To use virtual consoles, hold down the left ALT key and press one of the function keys F1 through F8. Each of those function keys will bring up a separate UNIX session with its own shell prompt. Use each one for whatever you want—just remember to log out from each virtual console when you're done!

We won't mention Linux virtual consoles any more. This chapter introduces the X Window System (called X for short), the most common UNIX window system. This introduction should also help you use non-X window systems.

Like UNIX, X is very flexible. The appearance of windows, the way menus work, and other features are controlled by a program called the *window manager.* Three common window managers are **mwm**, **fvwm**, and **twm**. There are plenty of other window managers—including **fvwm95**, which simulates a Windows 95 desktop on UNIX. This chapter explains **mwm** and uses it in examples. The details of using other window managers, and the ways they appear on the display, are somewhat different—but this chapter should help you use them, too.

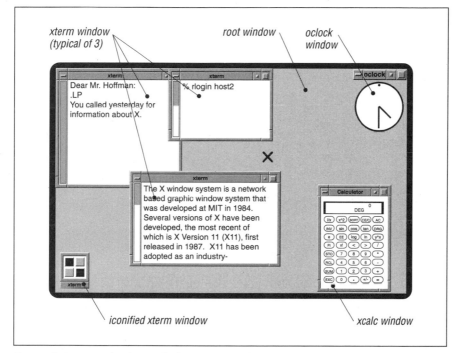

Figure 2-1: An X display with the mwm window manager

Starting X

There are several ways to start X and its window manager. This section explains a few of the most common ways. Figure 2-2 shows some steps along a few different paths to starting X. If your display is like any of the following, refer to the section noted. (If none of these fits your situation, skim through the next three sections or ask your system administrator for help.)

- Figure 2-2A, **xdm** is running. Start with Section A.

- Figure 2-2B, you have a standard UNIX login session. Start with Section B.

- Figure 2-2C, X is running but a window manager probably isn't. (You can tell because the window doesn't have a "frame" around it.) Read Section C.

- Figure 2-2D, the window has a frame, so X and the window manager (in this example, **mwm**) are running. You can skip ahead to the next main section, "Running Programs."

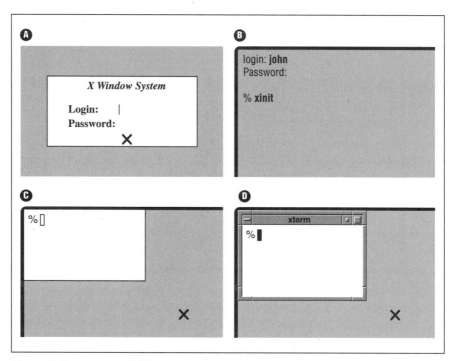

Figure 2-2: Some possibilities

A. Ready to Run X (with xdm)

Some terminals, like the one shown in Figure 2-2A, are probably ready to use X. Your terminal has probably been set up to use **xdm**, the X display manager; **xdm** logs you in to your UNIX host and (usually) starts the window manager.

When you start, there's a single window in the middle of the screen that says something like "X Window System on *hostname*." The window has two prompts, "Login:" and "Password:". A cursor (a vertical bar) sits to the right of the "Login:" line. Type your username (login name) and press RETURN . Do the same for your password. The login window disappears.

If a display something like Figure 2-1 or Figure 2-2D appears, You're ready to use X! You can skip ahead to "Running Programs."

If you get a display like Figure 2-2C, read Section C below. Or, if you get a blank display, try pressing and releasing your mouse buttons one by one, slowly, to see if a menu pops up.

B. Starting X from a Standard UNIX Session

If your terminal shows something like Figure 2-2B, with a standard UNIX "login:" prompt (not in a separate window; the whole screen looks like a terminal), then X is not running. Log in (as Chapter 1, *Getting Started*, explains) and get a shell prompt (like %). Next, you need to start X. The default command is:

```
% xinit
```

though your system may use another command (**startx**, for instance) instead. If all goes well, your screen will sprout at least one window. If the window looks like Figure 2-2C, without a frame from a window manager, read Section C. Otherwise, your window manager is running; skip ahead to the next main section, "Running Programs."

Problem checklist

No windows open. I got the message "Fatal server error: No screens found."
    Your terminal may not be able to run X. Ask the system administrator.

C. Starting the Window Manager

Once you have a window open with a shell prompt in it (usually % or $), you can start the window manager program. Your account may have been set up to do this automatically. If a window manager is not running, windows won't have frames (with titles, control boxes, and so on). Also, if you move the pointer to the root window (sometimes called the "desktop") and press the mouse buttons, menus won't appear unless the window manager is running.

If you need to start the window manager, move your pointer into the window. Then enter this command at the shell prompt to start the Motif window manager:

```
% mwm &
[1] 12345
%
```

(To start **twm**, **olwm**, or another window manager, the command you'd type would be the name of that window manager.) In a few moments, the window should have a frame. (For more about starting programs, refer to "The xterm Window" section, later in this chapter.)

Running Programs

One of the most important X features is that windows can come either from programs running on another computer or from an operating system other than UNIX. So, if your favorite MS-DOS program doesn't run under UNIX but has an X interface, you can run the program under MS-DOS and display its windows with X on your UNIX computer. Researchers can run graphical data analysis programs on supercomputers in other parts of the country and see the results in their offices. There's much more than we could cover here. The O'Reilly & Associates book *X Window System User's Guide, Volume Three, OSF/Motif Edition* has all the details.

Setting Focus

Of all the windows on your screen, only one window receives the keystrokes you type. This window is usually highlighted in some way. By default in the **mwm** window manager, for instance, the frame of the window that receives your input is a darker shade of grey. In X jargon, choosing the window you type to is called "setting the *input focus*." Most window managers can be configured to set the focus in one of the following two ways:

- Point to the window and click a mouse button (usually the first button). You may need to click on the titlebar at the top of the window.

- Simply move the pointer inside the window.

When you use **mwm**, any new windows will get the input focus automatically as they pop up.

The xterm Window

One of the most important windows is an **xterm** window. **xterm** makes a terminal emulator window with a UNIX login session inside, just like a miniature terminal. You can have several **xterm** windows at once, each doing something different. To enter a UNIX command or answer a prompt in a window, set the focus there and type. Programs in other windows will keep running; if they need input from you, they'll wait just as they would on a separate terminal.

Figure 2-2D and Figure 2-4 show a single **xterm** window with a shell prompt (%) inside. If you enter a UNIX command (like **date**), it will run just as it would on a non-window terminal.

You can also start separate X-based window programs (typically called *clients*) by entering commands in an **xterm** window. Although you can start new clients (**xterm**, **xcalc**, and so on) from any open **xterm** window on your computer, we recommend starting all of them from the first window that you opened. If you do that, and if your shell has job control (see Chapter 6, *Multitasking*), it's easy to find and control all the clients.

Here's an example. To start the calculator called **xcalc**, enter:

```
% xcalc &
[1] 12345
%
```

The shell will print a PID number like 12345. (Chapter 6 has more information on this subject.) If you forget to add the ampersand (&) at the end of the line, kill (terminate) **xcalc** with your interrupt character (like CTRL-C) to get another shell prompt—then enter the command correctly.

The new window may be placed and get the focus automatically. Or, the window (or an outline of it) may "float" above the display, following the pointer—until you point somewhere and click the mouse button to place the window.

You can also start a new **xterm** from an existing **xterm**. Just enter **xterm &** (don't forget the ampersand) at the shell prompt.

The same method works for starting other X programs.

The Root Menu

If you move the pointer onto the root window (the "desktop" behind the windows) and press the correct mouse button (usually the first or third button, depending on your setup), you should see the *root menu*. You may need to hold down the button to keep the menu visible. The root menu has commands for controlling windows. The menu's commands may differ depending on the system.

Your system administrator (or you, if you study your window manager) can add commands to the root menu. These can be window manager operations or commands to open other windows. For example, a "New Window" menu item can open a new **xterm** window for you. A "Calculator" item could start **xcalc**.

Exercise

Change to your home directory.	Enter **cd**
Open two **xterm** windows.	Enter **xterm &** twice or select that item twice on the root menu.
Practice setting focus on both new windows and entering UNIX commands in each.	Click on window and/or move pointer there. Enter **who am i**, etc.
Start the clock from one window.	Enter **oclock &**
Start the calculator from one window and try it.	Enter **xcalc &**
Change working directory (see Chapter 3) in only *one* window.	Enter **cd /bin**
Check working directory (see Chapter 3) in *both* windows.	Enter **pwd**
Terminate **xcalc**.	Set focus on the **xcalc**, and type your interrupt character (such as CTRL-C).

Problem checklist

When I try to start a client, I see "connection refused by server" or "client is not authorized to connect to server."

> You may need to run the **xhost** command. See your system administrator or an experienced X user.

When I try to start a client, I see "Error: Can't open display."
  Your DISPLAY environment variable may not be set correctly or you
  may need to use the **–display** option. Ask for help or refer to the *X
  Window System User's Guide, Volume 3*.

Working with a Mouse

Let's look at some basics of using a mouse or other pointing device.

Pointer Shape

As you move the mouse pointer* from the root window onto other windows or menus, the shape of the pointer will change. For instance, on the
root window, the pointer is a big X. The pointer may change to an hour-
glass shape to tell you to wait. When you resize a window, the pointer
changes to a cross with arrows.

Pointing, Clicking, and Dragging

What's "pointing and clicking"? That's when you move the pointer to a
place (usually over part of a window), then quickly press and release a
mouse button (usually the first button). It's the same idea as pressing a
button on a telephone or another electronic appliance.

Something else you'll do is "dragging." That means moving the pointer to
a place (such as the corner of a window), then pressing a mouse button
and holding it down while you move the pointer. This is called "dragging"
a pointer or object, because the object will be dragged along with the
pointer until you let go of the mouse button.

Using a Mouse with xterm Windows

Xterm windows have an advantage over plain UNIX terminals in that you
can copy and paste text within a window or between windows. To get
started, move the pointer inside an **xterm** window and select the window
(set the focus there). Notice that the pointer changes to an "I-beam"
shape. There's also a block cursor. As you type, notice that text you input
appears at the block-shaped cursor, just like it would on a standard terminal. So, think of the block cursor as the window's input point.

---

* The correct word for this symbol is *cursor*. But **xterm** and some other windows also have
separate cursors to show where text will be entered. To avoid confusion, we use the word
"pointer" for the cursor that moves all across the display under control of the mouse.

The I-beam pointer selects text for copying. Let's try it. Point to the first character of a command line (not the prompt) and click the first mouse button. Next, move the pointer to the end of the text you want to select and click the third button. The text between the first and third clicks should be highlighted. (If you accidentally click another button, you may need to start over.) Your **xterm** window should look something like Figure 2-3.

Next, click (don't hold) the second (middle) mouse button. The selected text will be copied into the window at the block cursor, just as if you had typed it in. Press RETURN to run the command line; otherwise, backspace over it to get back to the prompt.

You can also select text by clicking in an **xterm** window. Point to a word and double-click (click twice, quickly) the first button; the word should be highlighted. Point to a line and triple-click to highlight the whole line. You can select and copy any text, not just command lines.

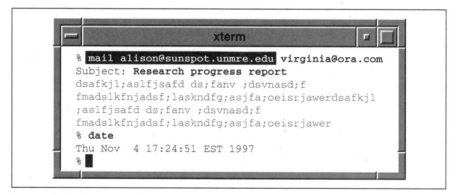

Figure 2-3: Copying and pasting a command line

The same copying and pasting works between **xterm** windows and between many other (but not all) windows that handle text. You can select text in one window and paste it into the other window. This is very handy for text editing.

Working with Windows

A window manager program helps you control windows. This section explains how **mwm** manages windows. Other window managers do the same kinds of things—but with some variation. Let's start by looking at Figure 2-4, a typical window under **mwm**.

The top part of every window has a *titlebar* with the title of the window and three buttons. The edges of the window can be used to resize the window. (See the Note in "Resizing Windows," later in this chapter.)

Using the Titlebar

The top part of a window has three buttons (see Figure 2-4).

The two buttons at the top right corner have boxes inside them. Clicking the button with the small box makes the window as small as possible; the window turns into an *icon*. "Iconifying" puts unneeded windows out of the way without quitting the program inside them; it also keeps you from accidentally typing into a window. (Figure 2-1 shows an icon.) The button with the big square *maximizes* a window. That makes it as big as the client will allow, often as big as the screen.

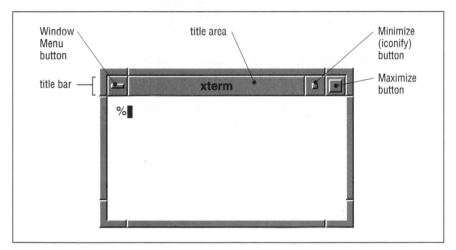

Figure 2-4: A window running with the Motif Window Manager

The left button opens the window menu; this is explained in "The Window Menu" section later in this chapter.

Moving Windows and Icons

To move a window, start by pointing to the titlebar. To move an icon, point to it. Hold down the first mouse button and drag to the new location—then let go of the button. You can also start the move from the window menu (see the following section on the window menu), but we think this way is easier.

Resizing Windows

If you have the pointer inside a window and then move the pointer to an edge, the pointer will change to an arrow shape. The arrow points the direction that you can resize the window. If you pointed to one of the corners, you can resize both sides that meet at the corner. To resize when you have the arrow pointer, press and hold the first button, then drag the window border until the window size is what you want and release the button. If you don't get quite the size you want, just do it again.

NOTE　　　On some versions of UNIX and with some programs, changing the size of an **xterm** window may confuse programs currently running in that window. Also, remember that many UNIX terminals are 80 characters wide; if you're editing text in a window and change its width to something other than 80 characters, that can cause trouble later when the file is viewed on a standard 80-character–wide terminal.

The Window Menu

Under **mwm**, each window can be controlled by its own *window menu*. There are lots of ways to get a window menu. Here are two: click on the menu button at the top left corner of a frame (Figure 2-4), or click on an icon. Figure 2-5 shows a window menu. When the menu pops up, you can point to one of the items and click it:

- **Restore** restores a minimized (icon) or maximized window to its original size. In Figure 2-5, the **Restore** entry is in a lighter typeface; this means you can't select it. (The window is already its normal size; restoring it wouldn't do anything.)

- **Move** lets you reposition a window on the screen.

- **Size** lets you change a window's size. (See the preceding Note.)

- The **Minimize** and **Maximize** operations are explained in "Using the Titlebar," earlier in this chapter.

- **Lower** moves a window to the bottom of the stack, if it's in a stack of windows.

- **Close** terminates the window and the program in it. Use this as a last resort. If the program has a separate menu or quit command (for example, entering **exit** at a shell prompt in an **xterm** window), use it instead of **Close**. (See "Quitting," later in this chapter, for explanation.)

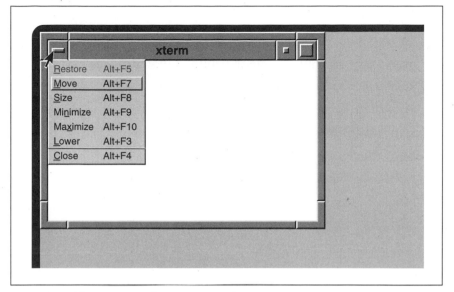

Figure 2-5: The mwm window menu

On the menu, a *keyboard shortcut* follows each command. You don't have to use the mouse to choose commands. For example, to **Minimize** (iconify) a window, hold down the ALT (or META) key and press the F9 key. The shortcut for bringing up the window menu (and taking it away) is to hold the SHIFT key and press the ESC (ESCAPE) key. If your keyboard doesn't have all of those keys, the menu can be customized to use different keys. O'Reilly & Associates' *X Window System User's Guide, Volume 3M*, explains how.

Exercise

Copy and paste part of a command line.	Type **who am i;date** and press RETURN in one **xterm** window. Highlight the **who am i**, set focus to the other **xterm** window, and copy the command there.
Move a window.	Grab and drag the window by its titlebar.
Iconify a window from the titlebar.	Use the Mimimize button.
Restore the icon.	Select **Restore** from the window menu.

Other X Clients

Here are a few of the X client programs that your system may have:

- **resize**: helps programs in **xterm** windows recognize new window size
- **xbiff**: tells you when new electronic mail comes in
- **xclipboard**: helps with copying and pasting text
- **xdpr**: prints a window (with the printer)
- **xedit**: simple text editor
- **xmag**: magnifies parts of the screen
- **xman**: browses UNIX manual (reference) pages
- **xmh**: electronic mail program
- **xset**: sets user preferences

For more information on those programs, see your online documentation or the O'Reilly *X Window System User's Guide.*

Quitting

Like almost everything in X, the way to quit X is configurable. The key to shutting down X is to know which of your programs (your windows or window manager) is the *controlling program.* When the controlling program quits, any leftover X programs are killed immediately. The controlling program is usually either the window manager or the single **xterm** window that started your X session.

Find the controlling program for your X session and write it down:

_____ Program to quit last

If your controlling program is an **xterm** window, we suggest leaving that window iconified from just after you've logged in until you've shut down all the other X clients. That way, you won't end your X session accidentally by closing that **xterm** window too soon.

To quit the window manager, select the **Exit** or **Quit** command on the root menu.

Here are the steps to shut down X:

1. Quit all noncontrolling programs (all programs *other* than the controlling program).

If any windows are running programs that have their own "quit" commands, it's a good idea to use those special commands to quit. For example, if you're running a text editor in an **xterm** window, use the editor's "quit" command, then finish the **xterm** window by entering **exit** at the shell prompt.

Using the program's own "quit" command gives the program time to clean up and shut down gracefully. On the other hand, the **Close** item on the **mwm** window menu can interrupt and kill a program before it's ready. If, however, a program doesn't have its own "quit" command, use **Close** on the window menu.

If any icons are running programs that have their own "quit" command, open the icons into windows and use the "quit" commands.

2. Quit the controlling program.

   After X shuts down, you may get a UNIX shell prompt. If you do, you can log out by entering **exit**. If you simply get another login box from **xdm** (as in Figure 2-2), you're done.

3

Your UNIX Account

Once you log in, you can use the many facilities UNIX provides. As an authorized system user, you have an account that gives you:

- A place in the UNIX filesystem where you can store your files.

- A username that identifies you and lets you control access to your files and receive messages from other users.

- A customizable environment that you can tailor to your preferences.

The UNIX Filesystem

A *file* is the unit of storage in UNIX, as in many other systems. A file can hold anything: text (a report you're writing, a to-do list), a program, digitally encoded pictures or sound, and so on. All of those are just sequences of raw data until they are interpreted by the right program.

In UNIX, files are organized into directories. A *directory* is actually a special kind of file where the system stores information about other files. A directory can be thought of as a place, so that files are said to be contained *in* directories and you are said to work *inside* a directory. (If you've used a Macintosh or Microsoft Windows computer, a UNIX directory is a lot like a folder. MS-DOS and UNIX directories are very similar.)

Your Home Directory

When you log in to UNIX, you're placed in a directory called your *home directory*. This home directory, a unique place in the UNIX filesystem, contains the files you use almost every time you log in. In your home directory, you can make your own files. As you'll see in a minute, you can also store your own directories within your home directory. Like folders in a file cabinet, this is a good way to organize your files.

Your Working Directory

Your *working directory* (sometimes called your current working directory) is the directory you're currently working in. At the start of every session, your home directory is your working directory. You may change to another directory, in which case the directory you move to becomes your working directory.

Unless you tell UNIX otherwise, all commands that you enter apply to the files in your working directory. In the same way, when you create files, they're created in your working directory.

The Directory Tree

All directories on a UNIX system are organized into a hierarchical structure that you can imagine as a family tree. The parent directory of the tree is known as the *root directory* and is written as a forward slash (/).

The root contains several directories. Figure 3-1 shows the top of an imaginary UNIX filesystem tree—the root directory and some of the directories under the root. *bin, etc, users, tmp,* and *usr* are some of the *subdirectories* (child directories) of *root.* These are fairly standard directories and usually contain specific kinds of system files. For instance, *bin* contains many UNIX commands. Not all systems have a directory named *users*; it may be called *u, home,* and/or be located in some other part of the filesystem.

In our example, the parent directory of *users* (one level above) is *root.* It also has two subdirectories (one level below), *john* and *carol.* On a UNIX system, each directory has one parent directory* and may have one or more subdirectories. A subdirectory (like *carol*) can have its own subdirectories (like *work* and *play*), to a limitless depth for practical purposes.

To specify a file or directory location, you write its *pathname.* A pathname is like the address of the directory or file in the UNIX filesystem. We'll look at pathnames in a moment.

---

* Q: Which directory doesn't seem to have a parent directory? **A:** On most UNIX systems, the root directory, at the top of the tree, is *its own* parent. Some systems have another directory above the root.

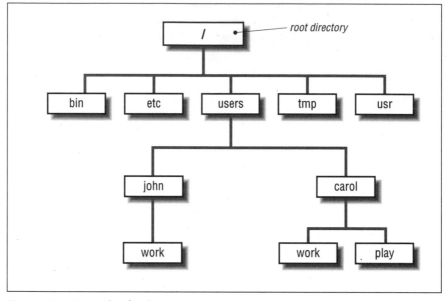

Figure 3-1: Example of a directory tree

On a basic UNIX system, all files in the filesystem are stored on disks connected to your computer. It isn't always easy to use the files on someone
else's computer or for someone on another computer to use your files.
Your system may have an easier way: a *networked filesystem* (with a name
like NFS or RFS). Networked filesystems make a remote computer's files
appear as if they're part of your computer's directory tree. For instance,
your computer in Los Angeles might have a directory named *boston*.
When you look in that subdirectory, you'll see some (or all) of the directory tree from your company's computer in Boston. Your system administrator can tell you if your computer has any networked filesystems.

Absolute Pathnames

As you saw above, the UNIX filesystem organizes its files and directories
in an inverted tree structure with the root directory at the top. An *absolute
pathname* tells you the path of directories you must travel to get from the
root to the directory or file you want. In a pathname, put slashes (/)
between the directory names.

For example, */users/john* is an absolute pathname. It locates just one directory. Here's how:

- the root is the first "/"
- the directory *users* (a subdirectory of *root*)
- the directory *john* (a subdirectory of *users*)

Be sure not to type spaces anywhere in the pathname. Figure 3-2 shows this structure.

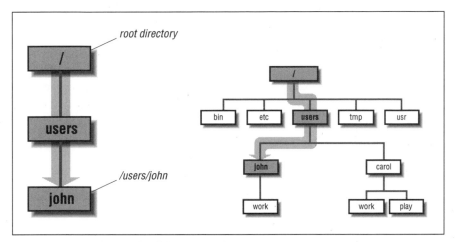

Figure 3-2: Absolute path of directory john

If you look at Figure 3-2, you'll see that the directory *john* has a subdirectory named *work*. Its absolute pathname is */users/john/work*.

The root is always indicated by the slash (/) at the start of the pathname.

Relative Pathnames

You can also locate a file or directory with a *relative pathname*. A relative pathname gives the location relative to your working directory.

Unless you use an absolute pathname (starting with a slash), UNIX assumes that you're using a relative pathname. Like absolute pathnames, relative pathnames can go through more than one directory level by naming the directories along the path.

For example, if you're currently in the *users* directory (see Figure 3-2), the relative pathname to the *carol* directory below is simply *carol*. The relative pathname to the *play* directory below that is *carol/play*.

Notice that neither of the pathnames in the previous paragraph starts with a slash. That's what makes them relative pathnames! These pathnames start at the working directory, not the root directory.

Exercise

Here's a short but important exercise. The example above explained the relative pathname *carol/play*. What do you think UNIX would say about the pathname */carol/play*? (Look again at Figure 3-2.)

UNIX would say "No such file or directory." Why? (Please think about that before you read more. It's very important and it's one of the most common beginner's mistakes.) Here's the answer. Because it starts with a slash, the pathname */carol/play* is an absolute pathname that starts from the root. It says to look in the *root* directory for a subdirectory named *carol*. But there is no subdirectory named *carol* one level directly below the root, so the pathname is wrong. The only absolute pathname to the *play* directory is */users/carol/play*.

Relative pathnames up

You can go up the tree by using the shorthand ".." (dot dot) for the parent directory. As you saw above, you can also go down the tree by using subdirectory names. In either case (up or down), separate each level by a slash (/).

Figure 3-3 shows a part of Figure 3-1. If your working directory in the figure is *work*, there are two pathnames for the *play* subdirectory of *carol*. You already know how to write the absolute pathname, */users/carol/play*. You can also go up one level (with "..") to *carol*, then go down the tree to *play*. Figure 3-3 shows that. The relative pathname would be *../play*. It would be wrong to give the relative address as *carol/play*. Using *carol/play* would say that *carol* is a subdirectory of your working directory instead of what it is in this case: the parent directory.

Absolute and relative pathnames are totally interchangeable. UNIX commands simply follow whatever path you specify to wherever it leads. If you use an absolute pathname, the path starts from the root. If you use a relative pathname, the path starts from your working directory. Choose whichever is easier at the moment.

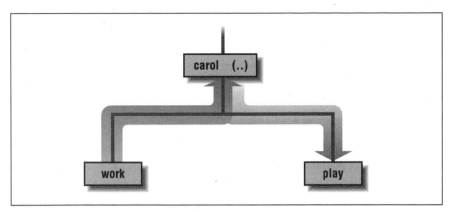

Figure 3-3: Relative pathname from work to play

Changing Your Working Directory

When you know the absolute or relative pathname of a directory, you can move up and down the UNIX directory tree.

pwd

To find which directory you're currently in, use the **pwd** (print working directory) command. The **pwd** command takes no arguments.

```
% pwd
/users/john
%
```

pwd prints the absolute pathname of your working directory.

cd

You can change your working directory to any directory (including another user's directory—if you have permission) with the **cd** (change directory) command.

The **cd** command has the form:

    cd *pathname*

The argument is an absolute or a relative pathname (whichever is easier) for the directory you want to change to.

```
% cd /users/carol
% pwd
/users/carol
% cd work
```

```
% pwd
/users/carol/work
%
```

Here's a handy tip: the command **cd**, with no arguments, takes you to your home directory from wherever you are in the filesystem.

Note that you can only change to another directory. You cannot **cd** to a filename. If you try, UNIX will give you an error message:

```
% cd /etc/passwd
/etc/passwd:  Not a directory
%
```

/etc/passwd is a file that contains information about users allowed to log in to the system.

Files in the Directory Tree

A directory can hold subdirectories. And, of course, a directory can hold files. Figure 3-4 is a close-up of the filesystem around *john*'s home directory. The four files are shown along with the *work* subdirectory.

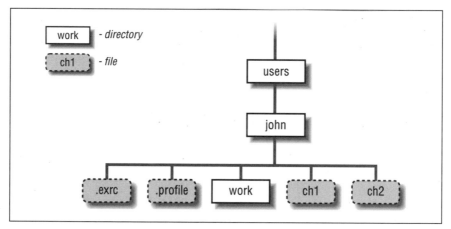

Figure 3-4: Files in the directory tree

Pathnames to files are made the same way as pathnames to directories. For example, if your working directory is *users*, the relative pathname to the *work* directory below would be *john/work*. The relative pathname to the *ch1* file would be *john/ch1*.

Listing Files

To use the **cd** command, you must decide which entries in a directory are subdirectories and which are files. The **ls** command lists the entries in the directory tree.

ls

When you enter the **ls** command, you'll get a listing of the files and subdirectories contained in your working directory. The syntax is:

> **ls** *option(s)* *directory-and-filename(s)*

If you've just logged in for the first time, entering **ls** without any arguments may seem to do nothing. This isn't surprising because you haven't made any files in your working directory. If you have no files, nothing is displayed; you'll simply get a new shell prompt.

```
% ls
%
```

But if you've already made some files or directories in your account, those names are displayed. The output depends on what's in your directory. The display should look something like this:

```
% ls
ch1    ch10   ch2    ch3    intro
%
```

(Some systems display filenames in a single column. If yours does, you can change the display to columns with the **–x** option.) **ls** has a lot of options that change the information and display format.

The **–a** option (for *all*) is guaranteed to show you some more files, as in the following example:

```
% ls -a
.      .exrc     ch1    ch2    intro
..     .profile  ch10   ch3
%
```

You'll always see at least two new entries with the names "." (dot) and ".." (dot dot). As mentioned earlier, .. is always the relative pathname to the parent directory, and a single . always stands for any working directory. There may also be other files, like *.profile* or *.exrc*. Any entry whose name begins with a dot is hidden—it will be listed only if you use **ls –a**.

To get more information about each file, add the –l option. (That's a lowercase letter "L" for *long*.) This option can be used alone, or in combina-
tion with –a, as shown in Figure 3-5.

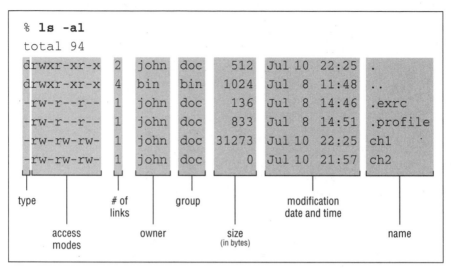

```
% ls -al
total 94
drwxr-xr-x  2  john  doc    512  Jul 10  22:25  .
drwxr-xr-x  4  bin   bin   1024  Jul  8  11:48  ..
-rw-r--r--  1  john  doc    136  Jul  8  14:46  .exrc
-rw-r--r--  1  john  doc    833  Jul  8  14:51  .profile
-rw-rw-rw-  1  john  doc  31273  Jul 10  22:25  ch1
-rw-rw-rw-  1  john  doc      0  Jul 10  21:57  ch2
```

type   # of   group   modification   name
               links   date and time

        access   owner   size
        modes   (in bytes)

Figure 3-5: Output from ls -al

The long format provides the following information about each file:

Total n

> *n* amount of storage used by the files in this directory.

Type

> Tells whether the file is a directory (**d**) or a plain file (–). (There are
> other less common types that we don't explain here.)

Access modes

> Specifies three types of users (yourself, your group, all others) who
> are allowed to read (**r**), write (**w**), or execute (**x**) your files.

Links

> The number of files and directories linked to this one.

Owner

> The person who created or owns the file.

Group

> The group that owns the file. (If your version of UNIX doesn't show
> this column, add the –g option to see it.)

Size (in bytes)
> The size of the file.

Modification date
> The date when the file was last modified.

Name
> The name of the file or directory.

Notice especially the columns that list the owner and group of the files, and the access modes (also called permissions). The person who creates a file is its owner; if you've created any files (or the system administrator did it for you), this column should show your username. You also belong to a group, to which you were assigned by the system administrator. Files you create will either be marked with the name of your group or, in some cases, the group that owns the directory.

The *permissions* control who can read, write (modify), or execute the file (if it's a program). The permissions have ten characters. The first character shows the file type (directory or plain file). The second through the fourth characters show the permissions for the file's owner—yourself if you created the file. The fifth through the seventh characters show permissions for other members of the file's group. The eighth through the tenth characters show permissions for all other users.

For example, the permissions for *.profile* are -rw-r--r--, so it's a plain file. You, the owner, have both read and write permissions. But other users of the system can only read the file; they cannot modify the file's contents. No one has execute (**x**) permission, which should only be used for executable files (files that hold programs).

In the case of directories, **x** means the permission to access the directory—for example, to run a command that reads a file there or to use a subdirectory. Notice that the two directories shown in the example are executable (searchable by you, by your group, and by everyone else on the system). A directory with **w** (write) permission allows deleting, renaming, or adding files within the directory. Read (**r**) permission allows listing the directory with **ls**.

You can use the **chmod** command to change the permissions of your files and directories. See the section of this chapter called "Protecting and Sharing Files."

If you need to know only which files are directories and which are executable files, you can use the **–F** option.

If you give the pathname to a directory, **ls** will list the directory but it will *not* change your working directory. The **pwd** command in the following example shows that:

```
% ls -F /users/andy
calendar    goals    ideas/
ch2         guide/   testpgm*
% pwd
/etc
%
```

ls −F puts a / (slash) at the end of each directory name. (The directory name doesn't really have a slash in it; that's just the shortcut **ls −F** uses with a directory.) In our example, *guide* and *ideas* are directories. You can verify this by using **ls −l** and noting the "d" in the first field of the output. Files with an execute status (**x**), like programs, are marked with an * (asterisk). The file *testpgm* is an executable file. Files that aren't marked are not executable.

On Linux and other systems with the GNU version of **ls**, you may be able to see names in color. For instance, directories could be green and program files could be yellow. Like almost everything on UNIX, of course, this is configurable—and the details are more than we can cover in an introductory book. Try typing **ls −−color** and see what happens. (It's time for our familiar mantra: "check your documentation"; see Chapter 7, *Where to Go From Here.*)

Exercise: Exploring the filesystem

You're now equipped to explore the filesystem with **cd**, **ls**, and **pwd**. Take a tour of the directory system, hopping one or many steps at a time, with a mixture of **cd** and **pwd** commands.

Go to your home directory.	Enter **cd**
Find your working directory.	Enter **pwd**
Change to new working directory.	Enter **cd /etc**
List files in new working directory.	Enter **ls**
Change directory to root and list files.	Enter **cd /; ls**
Change to a new directory.	Enter **cd usr**
Give a wrong pathname.	Enter **cd xqk**
Change to a new directory with its absolute pathname.	Enter **cd /etc**
List files in another directory.	Enter **ls /bin**

Find your working directory   Enter **pwd**
(notice that **ls** didn't change it).

Return to your home directory.   Enter **cd**

Looking Inside Files

By now, you're probably tired of looking at files from the outside. It's kind of like going to a bookstore and looking at the covers, but never getting to read a word. Let's look at three programs for reading files: **cat**, **more**, and **pg**.

cat

Most first-time users of UNIX think that **cat** is a strange name for a program. As we'll see later, **cat**, which is short for "concatenate," puts files together (concatenates them) to make a bigger file. It can also display files on your screen.

To display files on the standard output (your screen; see Chapter 5, *Redirecting I/O*), use:

     cat *file(s)*

For example, let's display the contents of the file */etc/passwd*. This system file describes users' accounts. (Your system may have a more complete list somewhere else.)

```
% cat /etc/passwd
root:x&k8KP30f;(:0:0:Root:/:
daemon:*:1:1:Admin:/:
           .
           .
           .
%
```

cat works best for short files containing one screenful or less. If you **cat** a file that is too long, it may roll up the screen faster than you can read it. You cannot go back to view the previous screens when you use **cat** (unless you're using an **xterm** window with a scrollbar, that is).

If you enter **cat** without a filename, get out by pressing RETURN followed by a single CTRL-D .

more

If you want to "read" a long file on the screen, your system may have the **more** command to display one screen or "page" of text at a time. A standard terminal screen can usually display 24 lines of text; a window can display almost any number of lines. The syntax is:

more *file(s)*

more lets you move forward in the files by any number of pages or lines. Most versions let you move backward, too. You can also move back and forth between two or more files specified on the command line. When you invoke **more**, the first "page" of the file appears on the screen. A prompt appears at the bottom of the screen, as in the following example:

```
% more ch03
A file is the unit of storage in UNIX as in many other systems.
A file can be anything: a program,
        .
        .
        .
--More--(47%)
```

The prompt says that you are 47% of your way through the file. The cursor sits to the right of this prompt as a signal for you to enter a **more** command to tell **more** what to do.

You can press "h" (for "help") at the **more** prompt to display the **more** commands available on your system. Table 3-1 lists some of the simpler (but quite useful) ones.

Table 3-1: Useful more Commands

Command	Description
SPACE	Display next page.
RETURN	Display next line.
*n*f	Move forward *n* pages.
b	Move backward one page.
*n*b	Move backward *n* pages.
/*word*	Search forward for *word*.
?*word*	Search backward for *word*.
v	Start the **vi** editor at this point.
CTRL-L	Redisplay current page.
h	Help.
:n	Go to next file on command line.

Table 3-1: Useful more Commands (continued)

:p	Go back to previous file on command line.
q	Quit **more** (before end of file).

pg

The **more** command isn't available on some UNIX systems. Most of those systems have the **pg** command instead. It works like **more** but has different features. For example, **pg** lets you move to specific lines.

The syntax is:

    pg *filename(s)*

If your system has **pg**, try it on a file that has more lines than your screen. Your screen displays the first page of the file. The last line is a colon (:) prompt. Press RETURN to view the next page or enter "q" to quit. Enter "h" for a list of **pg** commands.

Protecting and Sharing Files

UNIX makes it easy for users to share files and directories. Controlling exactly who has access takes some explaining, though—more explaining than we can do here. So here's a cookbook set of instructions. If you have critical security needs or you just want more information, see the references in Appendix A, *Reading List*.

Directory Access Permissions

A directory's access permissions help to control access to the files in it. These affect the overall ability to use files and subdirectories in the directory. (Once you have access to a directory, the ability to read or modify the contents of specific files is controlled by the file access permissions; see the second of the following two lists.)

In the commands below, replace *dirname* with the directory's pathname. An easy way to change permissions on the working directory is by using its relative pathname, . (dot), as in "**chmod 755 .**".

- To keep yourself from accidentally removing files (or adding or renaming files) in a directory, use **chmod 555** *dirname*. To do the same, but also deny other users any access, use **chmod 500** *dirname*.

- To protect the files in a directory and all its subdirectories from everyone else on your system—but still be able to do anything *you* want to dp there—use **chmod 700** *dirname*.

- To let other people on the system see what's in a directory—and read or edit the files if the file permissions let them—but not rename, remove, or add files—use **chmod 755** *dirname*.

- To let people in your UNIX group add, delete, and rename files in a directory of yours—and read or edit other people's files if the file permissions let them—use **chmod 775** *dirname*.

- To give full access to everyone on the system, use **chmod 777** *dirname*.

Remember, to access a directory, a user must also have execute (**x**) permission to all of its parent directories, all the way up to the root.

File Access Permissions

The access permissions on a file control what can be done to the file's *contents*. The access permissions on the *directory* where the file is kept control whether the file can be renamed or removed.

- To make a private file that only you can edit, use **chmod 600** *filename*. To protect it from accidental editing, use **chmod 400** *filename*.

- To edit a file yourself, and let everyone else on the system read it without editing, use **chmod 644** *filename*.

- To let you and all members of your UNIX group edit a file, but keep any other user from reading or editing it, use **chmod 660** *filename*.

- To let nongroup users read but not edit the file, use **chmod 664** *filename*.

- To let anyone read or edit the file, use **chmod 666** *filename*.

More Protection Under Linux

Most Linux systems have a command that gives you more choices on file and directory protection: **chattr**. **chattr** is being developed, and your version may not have all of the features that it will have in later versions of Linux. For instance, **chattr** can make a Linux file *append-only* (so it can't be overwritten, only added to); *compressed* (to save disk space automatically); *immutable* (so it can't be changed at all); *undeletable*, and more. Check your online documentation (type **man chattr**—see Chapter 7) or ask your system administrator for advice on your system.

Problem checklist

I get the message "chmod: Not owner."

Only the owner of a file or directory can set its permissions. Use **ls −l** to find the owner.

Electronic Mail

When you log in to your system, you may see a notice that says "You have mail." Someone has sent you a message or document by *electronic mail* (email). With email, you can compose a message at your terminal and send it to another user or list of users. You can also read any messages that others may have sent to you.

Email has several advantages over paper mail: it's convenient if you're already logged in, it's delivered much more quickly, you can send it to any number of people almost as easily as to just one person, and the messages can be stored for later reference.

There are a lot of email programs for UNIX. Some UNIX systems have only an old, simple program named **mail**, which this book doesn't cover. Most UNIX systems have a Berkeley program called **Mail** (with an uppercase "M"), **mailx**, or just **mail**. A popular menu-driven program that's easier to learn is called **pine**. All programs' basic principles are the same, though. We'll cover the Berkeley **mail** program.

Sending Mail

Your mail's recipient doesn't have to be logged in. The messages you send are stored in the recipient's "mailbox," a file deep in the UNIX filesystem (often located in the directory */usr/mail*). Messages are kept there until the recipient logs in and decides to read them.

To send mail, give the address of each person you want to send a message to, like this:

> **mail** *address1 address2* ...

There are several kinds of addresses, too many to explain here. If you have questions, see one of the references in Appendix A or ask your system administrator or postmaster (the person who maintains your email system). The most common addresses have this syntax:

> *username@hostname*

username is the person's username and *hostname* is the name of their computer. If the recipient reads email on the same computer you do, you may omit the *@hostname*. To keep a copy of your message, just add your username to the list of addresses.

After you enter **mail** and the addresses, in most cases the program (depending on how it's set up) will prompt you for the subject of the message. Type a one-line summary of the message (just like a paper memo) and press RETURN. Type in your message, line by line, pressing the RETURN key after every line, just as you would on a typewriter. When you have finished entering text, type CTRL-D (just once!) on a separate line. You should get the shell prompt at this point—though it might take a few seconds. If you change your mind before you type CTRL-D, you can cancel a message (while you are still entering text) by entering ˜q (a tilde character, then the letter "q") at the start of a line. The cancelled message is placed in a file called *dead.letter* in your home directory. To see other commands you can use while sending mail, enter ˜? (tilde question mark) at the start of a line of your message, then press RETURN. To redisplay your message after using ˜?, enter ˜p at the start of a line.

```
% mail alicia@moxco.chi.il.us
Subject: My trip to Chicago is on!
Alicia, I will be able to attend your meeting.
Please send me the agenda.  Thanks.
^D
%
```

You can't cancel a message after you type CTRL-D. (Unless you're a system administrator and you're lucky to catch the message in time, that is.) So, if you change your mind about Alicia's meeting, you'll need to send her another message.

Reading Your Mail

To read your mail, simply enter **mail** (or the name of your system's email command) at the shell prompt. You can do this at any time during the UNIX session, not just when you log in.

Let's read Jerry's message to Alicia:

```
% mail
Mail version SMI 4.0 Wed Oct 23 10:38:28 PDT 1991  Type ? for help.
"/usr/spool/mail/alicia": 2 messages 1 new
>U  1 bigboss        Sat May 22 06:56  19/529  In your spare time
 N  2 jpeek@jpeek.com Tue Nov  4 14:25  14/362  My trip to Chicago
& 2
```

```
Message 2:
Date: Tue, 4 Nov 1997 14:25:43 EST
From: jpeek@jpeek.com (Jerry Peek)
To: alicia@moxco.chi.il.us
Subject: My trip to Chicago is on!

Alicia, I will be able to attend your meeting.
Please send me the agenda.   Thanks.
& d
& q
Held 1 message in /usr/spool/mail/alicia
%
```

When you start **mail**, it prints a "message header" that shows whether each message is "new" (N) or "unread" (U), a message number, the sender, and when the message was sent. A ">" marks the current message. You can read any message by entering its number; if you use a command without a number, the command acts on the current message. If you read a message and don't delete it, the message is automatically moved to a file called *mbox* in your home directory.

The output of **mail** says that the message was sent by Jerry on Tuesday, November 4, at 2:25 p.m. The ampersand (&) on the last line is the **mail** program prompt. Just as the UNIX shell prompt is a sign that the shell is waiting for you to enter a command, the mail prompt is a sign that the **mail** program is waiting for you to enter a mail command. Your mail prompt may consist of a single character. Learn the mail prompt on your system and enter one of the commands in Table 3-2. For instance, Alicia might have chosen to enter **r** to reply to Jerry before using **d** to delete his message.

Table 3-2: Some mail Commands (at mail Prompt)

Command	Description
?	Display menu of mail commands.
#	Show message number #.
n	Display the next message.
p	Display current message.
d	Delete the message. Messages you read and don't delete are saved in *mbox*.
m *addrs*	Mail a message to the addresses *addrs*.
r	Reply to sender of current message.
R	Reply to sender and other recipients of current message.
s *file*	Save a message in the named *file*.

Table 3-2: Some mail Commands (at mail Prompt) (continued)

file *file*	Handle the messages in the named *file*.
file %	Handle the messages in your system mailbox.
h	Display summary of messages.
q	Quit the **mail** program.
x	Exit the **mail** program, ignoring any changes you made during this session.

Exercise: Sending mail

You can practice sending mail to your friends in this exercise. List the users logged on to the system and choose a name. You can also use your username to send mail to yourself. Enter the following message. Do not forget to press the RETURN key at the end of each line, and type CTRL-D on a line by itself when you're done.

List logged-on users.	Enter **who**
Send mail to someone.	Enter **mail** *name*
	Hi there!
	I'm just trying
	the mail program.
	^D

Changing Your Password

On most UNIX systems, everyone knows (or can find) your username. When you log in, how does the system decide that you are really the owner of your account—not an intruder trying to break in? It uses your password. If anyone knows both your username and password, they can probably use your account, and that includes sending mail that looks like you wrote it. So you should keep your password a secret!

If you think that someone knows your password, you should probably change it right away—although, if you suspect a computer "cracker" (or "hacker") is using your account to break into your system, ask your system administrator for advice first, if possible! You should also change your password periodically—every few months is recommended.

In general, a password should be something that's easy for you to remember but hard for other people (or password-guessing programs!) to guess. Your system should have guidelines for secure passwords. If it doesn't, here are some suggestions. A password should be between six and eight characters long. It should *not* be a word in *any* language, your phone number, your address, or anything that anyone else might know or guess that you'd use as a password. It's best to mix upper- and lower-case letters, punctuation, and numbers.

To change your password, you'll probably use either the *passwd* or *yppasswd* command. After you enter the command, it will prompt you to enter your current password ("old password"). If that's correct, it will ask you to enter your new password—twice, to be sure you don't make a typing mistake. For security, neither the old nor new passwords appear as you type them.

On some systems, your password change won't take effect for some time: from a few minutes to a day or so after you make it.

Customizing Your Account

As we saw earlier, your home directory may have a hidden file called *.profile*. If it doesn't, there'll probably be one or more files named *.login*, *.cshrc*, *.tcshrc*, *.bashrc*, *.bash_profile*, or *.bash_login*. These file are *shell setup files*, the key to customizing your account. Shell setup files contain commands that are automatically executed when a new shell starts—especially when you log in.

Let's take a look at these files. Go to your home directory, then use *cat* to display the file. Your *.profile* might look something like this:

```
PATH=/bin:/usr/bin:/usr/local/bin:
export PATH
/usr/games/fortune
date
umask 002
stty erase ^H intr ^C
```

A *.login* file might look something like this:

```
set path = (/bin /usr/bin /usr/local/bin .)
/usr/games/fortune
date
umask 002
stty erase ^H intr ^C
```

As you can see, these sample setup files contain commands to print a "fortune" and the date—just what happened earlier when we logged in! (*/usr/games/fortune* is a useless but entertaining program that prints a randomly selected saying from its collection. **fortune** isn't available on all systems.)

But what are these other commands?

- The line with `PATH=` or `set path` = tells the shell which directories to search for UNIX commands. This saves you the trouble of typing the complete pathname for each program you run. (Notice that */usr/games* isn't part of the path, so we had to use the absolute pathname to get our daily dose of wisdom from the **fortune** command.)

- The **umask** command sets the default file permissions assigned to all files you create. Briefly, a value of 022 sets the permissions `rw-r--r--` (read-write by owner, but read-only by everyone else), and 002 will produce `rw-rw-r--` (read-write by owner and group, but read-only by everyone else). If this file is a program or a directory, both **umasks** will also give execute (**x**) permission to all users. See one of the books in Appendix A or your UNIX documentation for details.

- The **stty** command sets your terminal control characters—for example, the erase and interrupt characters we discussed earlier.

You can execute any of these commands from the command line, as well. For example, to change your erase character from BACKSPACE (CTRL-H) to DEL (CTRL-?), you would enter:

```
% stty erase ^?
```

(The DEL key actually generates the control code CTRL-?, so that's what you'll see on your screen.)

Now pressing DEL will backspace and erase characters you type. (If your account is already set up to use DEL as the erase character, reverse this example, and change the erase character to BACKSPACE.)

If you experiment with **stty**, be careful not to reset the erase or interrupt character to a character you'll need otherwise. If you do, though, simply log out and then log back in; you'll get the default erase and interrupt characters again.

UNIX has many other configuration commands to learn about; the references in Appendix A list some of them. One popular configuration is to change your screen colors. On some Linux systems (and others), for example, the command **setterm -background blue** makes a blue background. Unfortunately, different systems do this in different ways; ask a local expert or someone who has a colored screen.

Just as you can execute the setup commands from the command line, the converse is true: any command that you can execute from the command line can be executed automatically when you log in by placing it in your setup file. (Running interactive commands like **mail** from your setup file isn't a good idea, though.)

You probably shouldn't edit your setup files yet, but it's good to know what's in them. Later, when you know more about UNIX, feel free to add or change commands in this file.

4

File Management

Methods of Creating Files

You'll usually create a text file with a text editor. An editor lets you add, change, and rearrange text easily. Two common UNIX editors are **vi** (pronounced "vee-eye") and **emacs** ("ee-macs").

Neither of those editors has the same features as popular word processing software on personal computers. Instead of being designed for making documents, envelopes, and so on, **vi** and **emacs** are very sophisticated, extremely flexible editors for all kinds of text files: programs, email messages, and so on. Many UNIX systems also support easy-to-use word processors. Ask your system administrator what's available. **Pico** is a simple editor (not word processor) that has been added to many UNIX systems.

Since there are several editor programs, you can choose one you're comfortable with. **vi** is probably the best choice because almost all UNIX systems have it, but **emacs** is also widely available. The O'Reilly & Associates books *Learning the vi Editor* and *Learning GNU Emacs* cover those editors in detail. If you'll be doing only simple editing, however, **pico** is a great choice. Although **pico** is much less powerful than **emacs** or **vi**, it's also a lot easier to learn.

You can also create a file by using a UNIX feature called *input/output redirection*, as Chapter 5, *Redirecting I/O*, explains. This sends the output of a command directly to a file—to make a new file or make an existing file larger.

File and Directory Names

As Chapter 3, *Your UNIX Account*, explained, both files and directories are identified by their names. A directory is really just a special kind of file, so the rules for naming directories are the same as the rules for naming files.

Filenames may contain any character except /, which is reserved as the separator between files and directories in a pathname. Filenames are usually made of upper- and lowercase letters, numbers, "." (dot), and "_" (underscore). Other characters (including spaces) are legal in a filename—but they can be hard to use because the shell gives them special meanings. So we recommend using only letters, numbers, dot, and underscore characters.

Unlike some operating systems, UNIX doesn't require a dot (.) in a filename; in fact, you can use as many as you want. For instance, the filenames *pizza* and *this.is.a.mess* are both legal.

Some UNIX systems limit filenames to 14 characters. Most newer systems allow much longer filenames.

A filename must be unique inside its directory, but other directories may have files with the same names. For example, you may have the files called *chap1* and *chap2* in the directory */users/carol/work* and also have files with the same names in */users/carol/play*.

File and Directory Wildcards

When you have a number of files named in series (for example, *chap1* to *chap12*) or filenames with common characters (like *aegis, aeon,* and *aerie*), you can use *wildcards* (also called *metacharacters*) to specify many files at once. These special characters are * (asterisk), ? (question mark), and [ ] (square brackets). When used in a filename given as an argument to a command:

* An asterisk is replaced by any number of characters in a filename. For example, *ae** would match *aegis, aerie, aeon,* etc. if those files were in the same directory. You can use this to save typing for a single filename (for example, *al** for *alphabet.txt*) or to name many files at once (as in *ae**).

? A question mark is replaced by any single character (so *h?p* matches *hop* and *hip,* but not *help*).

[ ]   Square brackets can surround a choice of characters you'd like to match. Any one of the characters between the brackets will be matched. For example, *[Cc]hapter* would match either *Chapter* or *chapter*, but *[ch]apter* would match either *capter* or *hapter*. Use a hyphen (−) to separate a range of consecutive characters. For example, *chap[1–3]* would match *chap1*, *chap2*, or *chap3*.

The examples below demonstrate the use of wildcards. The first command lists all the entries in a directory, and the rest use wildcards to list just some of the entries. The last one is a little tricky; it matches files whose names contain two (or more) *a*'s.

```
% ls
chap10          chap2           chap5           cold
chap1a.old      chap3.old       chap6           haha
chap1b          chap4           chap7           oldjunk
% ls chap?
chap2     chap5     chap7
chap4     chap6
% ls chap[5-8]
chap5     chap6     chap7
% ls chap??
chap10    chap1b
% ls *old
chap1a.old      chap3.old       cold
% ls *a*a*
chap1a.old      haha
```

Wildcards are useful for more than listing files. Most UNIX commands accept more than one filename, and you can use wildcards to put multiple files on the command line. For example, the command **more** is used to display a file on the screen. Let's say you want to display files *chap3.old* and *chap1a.old*. Instead of specifying these files individually, you could enter the command as:

```
% more *.old
```

This is equivalent to "**more chap1a.old chap3.old**".

Wildcards match directory names, too. For example, let's say you have subdirectories named *Jan*, *Feb*, *Mar*, and so on. Each has a file named *summary*. You could read all the summary files by typing "**more */summary**". That's almost equivalent to "**more Jan/summary Feb/summary** ..." but there's one important difference: The names will be alphabetized, so *Apr/summary* would be first in the list.

Managing Your Files

The tree structure of the UNIX filesystem makes it easy to organize your files. After you make and edit some files, you may want to copy or move files from one directory to another, rename files to distinguish different versions of a file, or give several names to the same file. You may want to create new directories each time you start working on a different project.

A directory tree can get cluttered with old files you don't need. If you don't need a file or a directory, delete it to free storage space on the disk. The sections below explain how to make and remove directories and files.

Creating Directories

It's handy to group related files in the same directory. If you were writing a spy novel, you probably wouldn't want your intriguing files mixed with restaurant listings. You could create two directories: one for all the chapters in your novel (*spy*, for example), and another for restaurants (*boston.dine*).

mkdir

To create a new directory, use the **mkdir** command. The format is:

> mkdir *dirname(s)*

dirname is the name of the new directory. To make several directories, put a space between each directory name. To continue our example, you would enter:

> % **mkdir spy boston.dine**

Copying Files

If you're about to edit a file, you may want to save a copy of it first. Doing that makes it easy to get back the original version.

cp

The **cp** command can put a copy of a file into the same directory or into another directory. **cp** doesn't affect the original file, so it's a good way to keep an identical backup of a file.

To copy a file, use the command:

> cp *old new*

where *old* is a pathname to the original file and *new* is the pathname you want for the copy. For example, to copy the */etc/passwd* file into a file called *password* in your working directory, you would enter:

```
% cp /etc/passwd password
%
```

You can also use the form:

> **cp** *old olddir*

This puts a copy of the original file *old* into an existing directory *olddir*. The copy will have the same filename as the original.

If there's already a file with the same name as the copy, **cp** will replace the old file with your new copy. This is handy when you want to replace an old copy with a newer version, but it can cause trouble if you accidentally overwrite a copy you wanted to keep. To be safe, use **ls** to list the directory before you make a copy there. Also, many versions of **cp** have a **−i** (interactive) option that will query the user before overwriting an existing file.

You can copy more than one file at a time to a single directory by listing the pathname of each file you want copied, with the destination directory at the end of the command line. You can use relative or absolute pathnames (see Chapter 3) as well as simple filenames. For example, let's say your working directory was */users/carol* (from the filesystem diagrams in Chapter 3). To copy three files called *ch1*, *ch2*, and *ch3* from */users/john* to a subdirectory called *work* (that's */users/carol/work*), by entering:

```
% cp ../john/ch1 ../john/ch2 ../john/ch3 work
```

Or, you could use wildcards and let the shell find all the appropriate files. This time, let's add the **−i** option for safety:

```
% cp -i ../john/ch[1-3] work
cp: overwrite work/ch2? n
```

There was already a file named *ch2* in the *work* directory. When **cp** asked, I answered **n** to prevent copying *ch2*. Answering **y** would overwrite the old *ch2*.

The shorthand forms . and .. will put the copy in the working directory or its parent. For example:

```
% cp ../john/ch[1-3] .
```

puts the copies into the working directory.

Problem checklist

The system says something along the lines of "cp: cannot copy file to itself".
> If the copy is in the same directory as the original, the filenames must be different.

The system says something like "cp: filename: no such file or directory".
> The system can't find the file you want to copy. Check for a typing mistake. If a file isn't in the working directory, be sure to use its pathname.

The system says something like "cp: permission denied".
> You may not have permission to copy a file created by someone else or copy it into a directory that does not belong to you. Use **ls −l** to find the owner and the permissions for the file, or **ls −ld** to check the directory. If you feel that you should have permission to copy a file whose access is denied to you, ask the file's owner or the system administrator to change the access modes for the file.

rcp

Some versions of UNIX have an **rcp** (remote copy) command for copying files between two computers. In general, you must have accounts on both computers. The syntax of **rcp** is like **cp**, but **rcp** also lets you add the remote hostname to the start of a file or directory pathname. The syntax of each argument is:

> *hostname:pathname*

hostname: is needed only for remote files. You can copy from a remote computer to the local computer, from the local to a remote, or between two remote computers.

For example, let's copy the files named *report.may* and *report.june* from your home directory on the computer named *giraffe*. Put the copies into your working directory (.) on the machine you're logged in to now:

```
% rcp giraffe:report.may giraffe:report.june .
```

To use wildcards in the remote filenames, put quotation marks ("*name*") around each remote name. For example, to copy all files from your *food/lunch* subdirectory on your *giraffe* account into your working directory on the local account, enter:

```
% rcp "giraffe:food/lunch/*" .
```

Unlike **cp**, most versions of **rcp** do not have a −i safety option. Also, even if your system has **rcp**, your system administrator may not want you to use it for system security reasons. Another command, **ftp**, is more flexible and secure than **rcp**.

ftp

The command **ftp** (file transfer protocol) is a flexible way to copy files between two computers. (Some systems have a friendlier version of **ftp** named **ncftp**.) Both computers don't need to be running UNIX, though they do need to be connected by a network (like the Internet) that **ftp** can use. To start **ftp**, give the hostname of the remote computer:

> **ftp** *hostname*

ftp will prompt for your username and password on the remote computer. This is something like a remote login (see Chapter 1, *Getting Started*), but **ftp** doesn't start your usual shell. Instead, **ftp** prints its own prompt and uses a special set of commands for transferring files. Table 4-1 lists the most important **ftp** commands.

Table 4-1: Some ftp Commands

Command	Description
put *filename*	Copies the file *filename* from your local computer to the remote computer. If you give a second argument, the remote copy will have that name.
mput *filenames*	Copies the named files (you can use wildcards) from local to remote.
get *filename*	Copies the file *filename* from the remote computer to your local computer. If you give a second argument, the local copy will have that name.
mget *filenames*	Copies the named files (you can use wildcards) from remote to local.
cd *pathname*	Changes the working directory on the remote machine to *pathname* (**ftp** usually starts at your home directory on the remote machine).
lcd *pathname*	Changes **ftp**'s working directory on the local machine to *pathname* (**ftp** starts at your working directory on the local computer). Note that the **ftp lcd** command changes only **ftp**'s working directory. After you quit **ftp**, your shell's working directory will not have changed.
dir	Lists the remote directory (like **ls −l**).
binary	Tells **ftp** to copy the following file(s) without translation. This preserves pictures, sound, or other data.

Table 4-1: Some ftp Commands (continued)

Command	Description
ascii	Transfers plain text files, translating data if needed.
quit	Ends the **ftp** session and takes you back to a shell prompt.

Here's an example. Carol uses **ftp** to copy the file *todo* from her *work* sub-directory on her account on the remote computer *rhino*:

```
% ls
afile    ch2     somefile
% ftp rhino
Connected to rhino.zoo.com.
Name (rhino:carol): csmith
Password:
ftp> cd work
ftp> dir
total 3
-rw-r--r--  1 csmith    mgmt     47 Feb  5  1997 for.ed
-rw-r--r--  1 csmith    mgmt    264 Oct 11 12:18 message
-rw-r--r--  1 csmith    mgmt    724 Nov 20 14:53 todo
ftp> get todo
ftp> quit
% ls
afile    ch2     somefile    todo
```

We've covered the most basic **ftp** commands here. Entering **help** at an `ftp>` prompt gives a list of all commands; entering **help** followed by an **ftp** command name gives a one-line summary of that command.

Renaming and Moving Files

You may need to change a filename. To rename a file, use the **mv** (move) command. The **mv** command can also move a file from one directory to another.

mv

The **mv** command has the same syntax as the **cp** command:

> mv *old new*

old is the old name of the file and *new* is the new name. **mv** will write over existing files, which is handy for updating old versions of a file. If you don't want to overwrite an old file, be sure that the new name is unique. If your **cp** has a −i option for safety, your **mv** probably has one too.

```
% mv chap1 intro
%
```

The previous example changed the name of the file *chap1* to *intro*. If you list your files with **ls**, you will see that the filename *chap1* has disappeared.

The **mv** command can also move a file from one directory to another. As with the **cp** command, if you want to keep the same filename, you only need to give **mv** the name of the destination directory.

Finding Files

If your account has lots of files, organizing those files into subdirectories can help you find the files later. Sometimes you may not remember which subdirectory has a file. The **find** command can search for files in many ways; we'll look at two of them.

Change to your home directory so **find** will start its search there. Then carefully enter one of the two **find** commands below. (The syntax is strange and ugly—but **find** does the job!)

```
% cd
% find . -type f -name 'chap*' -print
./chap2
./old/chap10b
% find . -type f -mtime -2 -print
./work/to_do
```

The first command looked in your working (home) directory and all its subdirectories for files (**-type f**) whose names start with *chap*. (**find** understands wildcards in filenames.) The second command looked for all files that have been created or modified in the last two days (**–mtime –2**). The relative pathnames that **find** finds start with a dot (*./*), the name of the working directory, which you can ignore.

Linux systems, and some others, have the GNU **locate** command. If it's been set up and maintained on your system, you can use **locate** to search part or all of a filesystem for a file with a certain name. For instance, if you're looking for a file named *alpha-test*, *alphatest*, or something like that, try this:

```
% locate alpha
/users/alan/alpha3
/usr/local/projects/mega/alphatest
```

You'll get the absolute pathnames of files and directories that have *alpha* in their names. (If you get a lot of output, add a pipe to **more** or **pg**—see

Chapter 5.) **locate** may or may not list protected, private files; its listings usually also aren't completely up to date. To learn much more about **find** and **locate**, read your online documentation (see Chapter 7, *Where to Go From Here*) or read the chapter about them in O'Reilly's *UNIX Power Tools*.

Removing Files and Directories

You may have finished working on a file or directory and see no need to keep it, or the contents may be obsolete. Periodically removing unwanted files and directories will free storage space.

rm

The **rm** command removes files. The syntax is simple:

> rm *filename(s)*

rm removes the named files, as the following examples show:

```
% ls
chap10       chap2       chap5    cold
chap1a.old   chap3.old   chap6    haha
chap1b       chap4       chap7    oldjunk
% rm *.old chap10
% ls
chap1b       chap4       chap6    cold    oldjunk
chap2        chap5       chap7    haha
% rm c*
% ls
haha     oldjunk
%
```

When you use wildcards with **rm**, be sure you're deleting the right files! If you accidentally remove a file you need, you can't recover it unless you have a copy in another directory or in the system backups.

CAUTION Do not enter **rm *** carelessly. It deletes all the files in your working directory.

Here's another easy mistake to make: You want to enter a command like **rm c*** (remove all filenames starting with "c") but instead enter **rm c *** (remove the file named **c** and all files!).

It's good practice to list the files with **ls** before you remove them. Or, if you use **rm**'s **–i** (*i*nteractive) option, **rm** will ask you whether you want to remove each file.

---

rmdir

Just as you can create new directories, you can also remove them with the **rmdir** command. As a precaution, the **rmdir** command will not let you delete directories that contain any files or subdirectories: the directory must first be empty. (The **rm −r** command removes a directory and everything in it. It can be dangerous for beginners, though.)

The syntax is:

> **rmdir** *dirname(s)*

If a directory you try to remove does contain files, you will get a message like "rmdir: *dirname* not empty".

To delete a directory that contains some files:

1. Enter **cd** *dirname* to get into the directory you want to delete.

2. Enter **rm *** to remove all files in that directory.

3. Enter **cd ..** to go to the parent directory.

4. Enter **rmdir** *dirname* to remove the unwanted directory.

Problem checklist

I still get the message "dirname not empty" even after I've deleted all the files.

> Use **ls −a** to check that there are no hidden files (names that start with a period) other than **.** and **..** (the working directory and its parent). The command **rm .[a−zA−Z] .??*** is good for cleaning up hidden files.

Files on Other Operating Systems

You read above about **ftp**, a program for transferring files across a network—possibly to non-UNIX operating systems. Your system may also be able to run operating systems other than UNIX. For instance, many Linux systems can also run MS-DOS and Windows 95. If yours does, you can probably use those files from your Linux account.

If the DOS or Windows filesystem is *mounted* with your other filesystems, you'll be able to use its files by typing a UNIX-like pathname. For instance, from our PC under Linux, we can access the DOS file *C:\WORD\REPORT.DOC* through the pathname */dosc/word/report.doc*.

Your Linux (or other) system may also have the MTOOLS utilities. These give you DOS-like commands that interoperate with the UNIX-like system. For example, we can put a Windows 95 floppy disk in the A: drive and then copy a file named named *summary.txt* into our current directory (.) by entering:

```
% mcopy a:summary.txt .
Copying summary.txt
%
```

Your system administrator should be able to tell you whether other filesystems are mounted, whether you have utilities like MTOOLS, and how to use them.

Printing Files

Before you print a file on a UNIX system, you may want to reformat it to adjust the margins, highlight some words, and so on. Most files can also be printed without reformatting, but the raw printout may not look quite as nice.

Many versions of UNIX include two powerful text formatters, **nroff** and **troff**. (There are also versions called **gnroff** and **groff**.) They are much too complex to describe here. Before we cover printing itself, let's look at a simple formatting program called **pr**.

pr

The **pr** command does minor formatting of files on the terminal screen or for a printer. For example, if you have a long list of names in a file, you can format it onscreen into two or more columns.

The syntax is:

pr *option(s) filename(s)*

pr changes the format of the file only on the screen or on the printed copy; it doesn't modify the original file. Table 4-2 lists some **pr** options.

Table 4-2: Some pr Options

Option	Description
−*k*	Produces *k* columns of output.
−d	Double-spaces the output (not on all **pr** versions).
−h *"header"*	Takes the next item as a report *header*.
−t	Eliminates printing of header and top/bottom margins.

Other options allow you to specify the width of the columns, set the page length, and so on.

Before using **pr**, here are the contents of a sample file named *food*:

```
% cat food
Sweet Tooth
Bangkok Wok
Mandalay
Afghani Cuisine
Isle of Java
Big Apple Deli
Sushi and Sashimi
Tio Pepe's Peppers
        .
        .
        .
```

Let's use **pr** options to make a two-column report with the header "Restaurants."

```
% pr -2 -h "Restaurants" food

Nov  7  9:58 1997  Restaurants    Page 1

Sweet Tooth                     Isle of Java
Bangkok Wok                     Big Apple Deli
Mandalay                        Sushi and Sashimi
Afghani Cuisine                 Tio Pepe's Peppers
              .
              .
              .

%
```

The text is output in two-column pages. The top of each page has the date and time, header (or name of the file, if header is not supplied), and page number. To send this output to the printer instead of the terminal screen, you create a pipe to the printer program—usually **lp** or **lpr**. The following section describes **lp** and **lpr**; Chapter 5 covers pipes.

lp and lpr

If you have a long file, it may be best to print it so you can see it all on paper. The command **lp** or **lpr** prints a file (onto paper as opposed to the screen display). Your system will probably have one or the other—but not both. The syntax is:

> **lp** *option(s) filename(s)*
> **lpr** *option(s) filename(s)*

Printers on UNIX systems are usually shared by a group of users. After you enter the command to print a file, the shell prompt returns to the screen and you can enter another command. However, seeing the prompt doesn't mean that your file has been printed. Your file has been added to the printer queue to be printed in turn.

Your system administrator has probably set up a default printer at your site. To print a file named *bills* on the default printer, use the **lp** or **lpr** command, as in this example:

```
% lp bills
request id is laserp-525   (1 file)
%
```

lp shows an ID that you can use to cancel the print job or check its status. If you need ID numbers for **lpr** jobs, use the **lpq** command (see "lpstat and lpq" in the following section). The file *bills* will be sent to a printer called *laserp*. The ID number of the request is "laserp-525".

lp and **lpr** have several options. Table 4-3 lists three of them.

Table 4-3: Some lp and lpr Options

Option		Description
lp	*lpr*	
−d*printer*	−P*printer*	Use given *printer* name if there is more than one printer at your site. The printer names are assigned by the system administrator.
−n#	−#	Print # copies of the file.
−m	−m	Notify sender by email when the printing is done.

If **lp** and **lpr** don't work at your site, ask other users for the printer command. You'll also need the printer locations—so you know where to get your output.

Problem checklist

My printout hasn't come out.

> See whether the printer is printing now. If it is, other users may have made a request to the same printer ahead of you and your file should be printed in turn. The section below explains how to check the print requests.

> If no file is printing, check the printer's physical connections and power switch. The printer may also be hung. If it is, ask your system administrator what to do.

Viewing the Printer Queue

If you want to find out how many files or "requests" for output are ahead of yours in the printer queue, use the command **lpstat** (for **lp**) or **lpq** (for **lpr**). The **cancel** command lets you terminate a printing request made by **lp**; **lprm** cancels jobs from **lpr**.

lpstat and lpq

The **lpstat** command shows what's in the printer queue: request IDs, owners, file sizes, when the jobs were sent for printing, and the status of the requests. Use **lpstat −o** if you want to see all output requests rather than just your own. Requests are shown in the order they'll be printed:

```
% lpstat -o
laserp-573   john   128865   Nov 7   11:27   on laserp
laserp-574   grace  82744    Nov 7   11:28
laserp-575   john   23347    Nov 7   11:35
%
```

The first entry shows that the request "laserp-573" is currently printing on *laserp*. The exact format and amount of information given about the printer queue may differ from system to system. If the printer queue is empty, **lpstat** will say "No entries" or simply give you back the shell prompt.

lpq gives slightly different information than **lpstat −o**:

```
% lpq
laserp is ready and printing
Rank     Owner    Job   Files               Total Size
active   john     573   report.ps           128865 bytes
1st      grace    574   ch03.ps ch04.ps     82744 bytes
2nd      john     575   standard input      23347 bytes
%
```

The first line displays the printer status. If the printer is disabled or out of paper, you may see different messages on this first line. The "active" job, the one being printed, is listed first. The "Job" number is like the **lpstat** request ID. To specify another printer, and the **−P** option (Table 4-3).

cancel and lprm

cancel terminates a printing request from the **lp** command. **lprm** terminates **lpr** requests. You can specify either the ID of the request (displayed by **lp** or **lpq**) or the name of the printer.

If you don't have the request ID, get it from **lpstat** or **lpq**. Then use **cancel** or **lprm**. Specifying the request ID·cancels the request, even if it is currently printing:

```
% cancel laserp-575
request "laserp-575" cancelled
```

To cancel whatever request is currently printing, regardless of its ID, simply enter **cancel** and the printer name:

```
% cancel laserp
request "laserp-573" cancelled
```

The **lprm** command will cancel the active job if it belongs to you. Otherwise, you can give job numbers as arguments, or use a dash (–) to remove all of your jobs:

```
% lprm 575
dfA575diamond dequeued
cfA575diamond dequeued
```

lprm tells you the actual filenames removed from the printer queue (which you probably don't need).

Exercise: Manipulating files

In this exercise, you'll create, rename and delete files. Find out if your site has one or more printers as well as the appropriate command to use for printing.

Go to home directory.	Enter **cd**
Copy distant file to working directory.	Enter **cp /etc/passwd myfile**
Create new directory.	Enter **mkdir temp**
List working directory.	Enter **ls -F**
Move file to new directory.	Enter **mv myfile temp**
Change working directory.	Enter **cd temp**
Copy file to working directory.	Enter **cp myfile myfile.two**
Print the file.	Enter your printer command and the filename
List filenames with wildcard.	Enter **ls -l myfile***
Remove files.	Enter **rm myfile***
Go up to parent directory.	Enter **cd ..**

Remove directory.	Enter **rmdir temp**
Verify that directory was removed.	Enter **ls -F**

5

Redirecting I/O

Standard Input and Standard Output

Many UNIX commands read input (such as a file) and write output.

In general, if no filename is specified in a command, the shell takes whatever you type on your keyboard as input to the command (after you press the first RETURN to start the command running, that is). Your terminal keyboard is the command's *standard input*.

As a command runs, the results are usually displayed on your terminal screen. The terminal screen is the command's *standard output*.

So, by default, each command takes its input from the standard input and sends the results to the standard output.

These two default cases of input/output can be varied. This is called *input/output redirection*. You can use a given file as input to a command that doesn't normally accept filenames by using the "<" (less-than symbol) operator. For example, the following command mails the contents of the file *to_do* to *bigboss@corp*:

```
% mail bigboss@corp < to_do
%
```

You can also write the results of a command to a named file or some other device instead of displaying output on the screen using the > (greater-than symbol) operator. The pipe operator | sends the standard output of one command to the standard input of another command. Input/output redirection is one of the nicest features of UNIX because of its tremendous power and flexibility.

Putting Text in a File

Instead of always letting the output of a command come to the screen, you can redirect output into a file. This is useful when you have a lot of output that would be hard to read on the screen or when you put files together to create a bigger file.

As we've seen, the **cat** command can display a short file. It can also be used to put text into a file, or to create a bigger file out of smaller files.

The > operator

When you add "> *filename*" to the end of a command line, the results of the command are diverted from the standard output to the named file. The > symbol is called the *output redirection operator.*

For example, let's use **cat** with this operator. The contents of the file that you'd normally see on the screen (from the standard output) are diverted into another file:

```
% cat /etc/passwd > password
% cat password
root::0:0:Root:/:/bin/sh
daemon:NONE:1:1:Admin:/:
            .
            .
            .
john::128:50:John Doe:/usr/john:/bin/sh
%
```

An example in Chapter 3, *Your UNIX Account,* showed how **cat** */etc/passwd* displays the file */etc/passwd* on the screen. The example above adds the > operator; so the output of **cat** goes to a file called *password* in the working directory. Displaying the file *password* shows that its contents are the same as the file */etc/passwd* (the effect is the same as the copy command **cp /etc/passwd password**).

You can use the > redirection operator with any command that sends text to its standard output—not just with **cat**. For example:

```
% who > users
% date > today
% ls
password    today    users    ...
```

We've sent the output of **who** to a file called *users* and the output of **date** to the file named *today*. Listing the directory shows the two new files. Let's look at the output from the **who** and **date** commands, regarding these two files:

```
% cat users
tim       tty1     Aug 12   07:30
john      tty4     Aug 12   08:26
% cat today
Tue Aug 12 08:36:09 EDT 1997
%
```

You can also use the **cat** command and the > operator to make a small text file. We told you earlier to type CTRL-D if you accidentally enter **cat** without a filename. This is because the **cat** command alone takes whatever you type on the keyboard as input. Thus, the command:

cat > *filename*

takes input from the keyboard and redirects it to a file. Try the following example:

```
% cat > to_do
Finish report by noon
Lunch with Xannie
Swim at 5:30
^D
%
```

cat takes the text that you typed as input, and the > operator redirects it to a file called *to_do*. Type CTRL-D on a new line by itself to signal the end of the text. You should get a shell prompt.

You can also create a bigger file out of many smaller files using the **cat** command and the > operator. The form:

cat *file1 file2* > *newfile*

creates a file *newfile*, consisting of *file1* followed by *file2*.

```
% cat today to_do > diary
% cat diary
Tue Aug 12 08:36:09 EDT 1997
Finish report by noon
Lunch with Xannie
Swim at 5:30
%
```

CAUTION   If you are using the > (output redirection) operator, you
              should be careful not to overwrite the contents of a file
              accidentally. Your system may let you redirect output to an
              existing file. If so, the old file will be deleted (or, in UNIX
              lingo, "clobbered"). Be careful not to overwrite a much-
              needed file! Many shells can protect you from this risk. In
              the C shell, use the command **set noclobber**. The Korn shell
              and **bash** command is **set –o noclobber**. Enter the com-
              mand at a shell prompt or put it in your shell's startup file.
              After that, the shell will not allow you to redirect onto an
              existing file and overwrite its contents.

              This doesn't protect against overwriting by UNIX com-
              mands like **cp**; it works only with the > redirection opera-
              tor. For more protection, you can set UNIX file access
              permissions.

The >> operator

You can add more text to the end of an existing file, instead of replacing
its contents, by using the >> (append redirection) operator. Use it like the
> (output redirection) operator. So,

> cat *file2* >> *file1*

appends the contents of *file2* to the end of *file1*. For an example, let's
append the contents of the file *users*, and also the current date and time,
to the file *diary*. Then we display the file:

```
% cat users >> diary
% date >> diary
% cat diary
Tue Aug 12 08:36:09 EDT 1997
Finish report by noon
Lunch with Xannie
Swim at 5:30
tim     tty1    Aug 12   07:30
john    tty4    Aug 12   08:26
Tue Aug 12 09:07:24 EDT 1997
%
```

Pipes and Filters

In addition to redirecting input/output to a named file, you can connect
two commands together so that the output from one program becomes
the input of the next program. Two or more commands connected in this
way form a *pipe*. To make a pipe, put a vertical bar (|) on the command
line between two commands. When a pipe is set up between two

commands, the standard output of the command to the left of the pipe symbol becomes the standard input of the command to the right of the pipe symbol. Any two programs can form a pipe as long as the first program writes to standard output and the second program reads from standard input.

When a program takes its input from another program, performs some operation on that input, and writes the result to the standard output (which may be piped to yet another program), it is referred to as a *filter*. One of the most common uses of filters is to modify output. Just as a common filter culls unwanted items, the UNIX filters can be used to restructure output.

Almost all UNIX commands can be used to form pipes. Some programs that are commonly used as filters are described below. Note that these programs aren't used only as filters or parts of pipes. They're also useful on their own.

grep

The **grep** program searches a file or files for lines that have a certain pattern. The syntax is:

> **grep** *pattern file(s)*

The name "grep" derives from the **ed** (a UNIX line editor) command **g/re/p** which means "globally search for a *regular expression* and *print* all lines containing it." A *regular expression* is either some plain text (a word, for example) and/or special characters used for pattern matching. When you learn more about regular expressions, you can use them to specify complex patterns of text. See *Mastering Regular Expressions*, by Jeffrey Friedl (O'Reilly & Associates, 1997), and the references in Appendix A.

The simplest use of **grep** is to look for a pattern consisting of a single word. It can be used in a pipe so that only those lines of the input files containing a given string are sent to the standard output. If you don't give **grep** a filename to read, it reads its standard input; that's the way all filter programs work:

```
% ls -l | grep "Aug"
-rw-rw-rw-   1 john   doc       11008 Aug  6 14:10 ch02
-rw-rw-rw-   1 john   doc        8515 Aug  6 15:30 ch07
-rw-rw-r--   1 john   doc        2488 Aug 15 10:51 intro
-rw-rw-r--   1 carol  doc        1605 Aug 23 07:35 macros
%
```

First, our example runs **ls** −**l** to list your directory. The standard output of **ls** −**l** is piped to **grep**, which only outputs lines that contain the string "Aug" (that is, files that were last modified in August). Because the standard output of **grep** isn't redirected, those lines go to the terminal screen.

grep options let you modify the search. Table 5-1 lists some of the options.

Table 5-1: Some grep Options

Option	Description
−v	Print all lines that do not match pattern.
−n	Print the matched line and its line number.
−l	Print only the names of files with matching lines (letter "l").
−c	Print only the count of matching lines.
−i	Match either upper- or lowercase.

Next, let's use a regular expression that tells **grep** to find lines with "carol", followed by zero or more other characters (abbreviated in a regular expression as ".*"), then followed by "Aug". For more about regular expressions, see the references in Appendix A, *Reading List.*

```
% ls -l | grep "carol.*Aug"
-rw-rw-r--   1 carol doc      1605 Aug 23 07:35 macros
%
```

sort

The **sort** program arranges lines of text alphabetically or numerically. The example below sorts the lines in the *food* file (from Chapter 4, *File Management*) alphabetically. **sort** doesn't modify the file itself; it reads the file and writes the sorted text to the standard output.

```
% sort food
Afghani Cuisine
Bangkok Wok
Big Apple Deli
Isle of Java
Mandalay
Sushi and Sashimi
Sweet Tooth
Tio Pepe's Peppers
```

sort arranges lines of text alphabetically by default. There are many options that control the sorting. Some of these are given in Table 5-2.

Table 5-2: Some sort Options

Option	Description
-n	Sort numerically (example: 10 will sort after 2), ignore blanks and tabs.
-r	Reverse the order of sort.
-f	Sort upper- and lowercase together.
+x	Ignore first x fields when sorting.

More than two commands may be linked up into a pipe. Taking a previous pipe example using **grep**, we can further sort the files modified in August by order of size. The following pipe consists of the commands **ls**, **grep**, and **sort**:

```
% ls -l | grep "Aug" | sort +4n
-rw-rw-r--  1 carol doc       1605 Aug 23 07:35 macros
-rw-rw-r--  1 john  doc       2488 Aug 15 10:51 intro
-rw-rw-rw-  1 john  doc       8515 Aug  6 15:30 ch07
-rw-rw-rw-  1 john  doc      11008 Aug  6 14:10 ch02
%
```

This pipe sorts all files in your directory modified in August by order of size, and prints them to the terminal screen. The **sort** option **+4n** skips four fields (fields are separated by blanks) then sorts the lines in numeric order. So, the output of **ls** (actually, the output of **grep**) is sorted by the file size (the fifth column, starting with 1605). Both **grep** and **sort** are used here as filters to modify the output of the **ls −l** command. If you wanted to email this listing to someone, you could add a final pipe to the **mail** command. Or you could print the listing by piping the **sort** output to your printer command (like **lp** or **lpr**).

pg and more

The **more** and **pg** programs that you saw earlier can also be used as filters. A long output would normally zip by you on the screen, but if you run text through **more** or **pg** as a filter, the display stops after each screenful of text.

Let's assume that you have a long directory listing. (If you want to try this example and need a directory with lots of files, use **cd** first to change to a system directory like */bin* or */usr/bin*.) To make it easier to read the sorted listing, pipe the output through **more**:

```
% ls -l | grep "Aug" | sort +4n | more
-rw-rw-r--  1 carol doc       1605 Aug 23 07:35 macros
-rw-rw-r--  1 john  doc       2488 Aug 15 10:51 intro
-rw-rw-rw-  1 john  doc       8515 Aug  6 15:30 ch07
```

```
-rw-rw-r--  1 john   doc      14827 Aug  9 12:40 ch03
     .
     .
     .
-rw-rw-rw-  1 john   doc      16867 Aug  6 15:56 ch05
--More--(74%)
```

The screen will fill up with one screenful of text consisting of lines sorted by order of file size. At the bottom of the screen is the **more** prompt where you can type a command to move through the sorted text. When you're done with this screen, you can use any of the commands listed in the discussion of the **more** program.

Exercise: Redirecting input/output

In the following exercises you'll redirect output, create a simple pipe, and use filters to modify output.

Redirect output to a file.	Enter **who > users**
Sort output of a command.	Enter **who	sort**
Append sorted output to a file.	Enter **who	sort >> users**
Display output to screen.	Enter **more users** or **pg users**
Display long output to screen.	Enter **ls -l /bin	more** or **ls -l /bin	pg**
Format and print a file with **pr**.	Enter **pr users	lp** or **pr users	lpr**

6

Multitasking

Suppose you are running a command that will take a long time to process. On a single-task system like MS-DOS, you would enter the command and wait for the system prompt to return, telling you that you could enter a new command. In UNIX, however, there is a way to enter new commands in the "foreground" while one or more commands are still running in the "background." This is called *background processing*.

When you enter a command as a background process, the shell prompt reappears immediately so that you can enter a new command. The original command will still be running in the background, but you can use the system to do other things during that time. Depending on your system and your shell, you may even be able to log off and let the background process run to completion.

Running a Command in the Background

Running a command as a background process is most often done to free a terminal when you know the command will take a long time to run.

To run a command in the background, add the "&" character at the end of the command line before you press the RETURN key. The shell will then assign and display a process ID number for the command:

```
% nroff -ms chap1 > chap1.out &
[1] 29890
%
```

(The **nroff** program formats documents. It's a good example because text formatting usually takes a while, so users often do it in the background. See your UNIX documentation for details on **nroff**.)

The process ID (PID) for this command is 29890. The PID is useful when you want to check the status of a background process or, if you need to, cancel it. You don't need to remember the PID, because there are UNIX commands (explained in later sections of this chapter) to check on the processes you have running. In some shells, a status line will be printed on your screen when the background process finishes.

In the C shell, you can put an entire sequence of commands separated by semicolons into the background by putting an ampersand at the end of the entire command line. In other shells, enclose the command sequence in parentheses before adding the ampersand:

> *(command1; command2)* &

On many systems, the shells have another feature called *job control*. You can use the *suspend character* (usually $\boxed{\text{CTRL-Z}}$) to suspend a program running in the foreground. The program will pause and you'll get a new shell prompt. You can then do anything else you like, including putting the suspended program into the background using the **bg** command. The **fg** command will bring a background process to the foreground.

For example, you might start **sort** running on a big file, and, after a minute, want to send email. You stop **sort**, then put it in the background. The shell prints a message, then another shell prompt. You send mail while **sort** runs.

```
% sort hugefile1 hugefile2 > sorted
       ...time goes by...
CTRL-Z  Stopped
% bg
[1]      sort hugefile1 hugefile2 > sorted &
% mail eduardo@nacional.cl
       . . .
```

Checking on a Process

If a background process takes too long, or you change your mind and want to stop a process, you can check the status of the process and even cancel it.

ps

When you enter the single-word command **ps**, you can see how long a process has been running. The output of **ps** also tells you the process ID of the background process and the terminal from which it was run.

```
% ps
PID      TTY      TIME    COMMAND
8048     020      0:12    sh
8699     020      0:02    ps
%
```

In its basic form, **ps** lists the following:

Process ID (PID)

A unique number assigned by UNIX to the process.

Terminal line (TTY)

The terminal number from which the process was started.

Run time (TIME)

The amount of computer time (in minutes and seconds) that the process has used.

Command (COMMAND)

The name of the process.

At the very least, **ps** will list one process: **ps** itself. You should also see the names of any other programs running in the background and the name of your shell's process (**sh**, **csh**, and so on).

You should be aware that there are two types of programs on UNIX systems: directly executable programs and interpreted programs. Directly executable programs are written in a programming language like C or Pascal and stored in a file that the system can read directly. Interpreted programs, such as shell scripts, are sequences of commands that are read by an interpreter program. If you execute an interpreted program, you will see an additional command (like **perl**, **sh**, or **csh**) in the **ps** listing, as well as any UNIX commands that the interpreter is executing now.

Shells with job control have a command called **jobs** which lists background processes started from that shell. As mentioned above, there are commands to change the foreground/background status of jobs. There are other job control commands as well. See the references in Appendix A, *Reading List*, for details.

Cancelling a Process

You may decide that you shouldn't have put a process in the background. Or you decide that the process is taking too long to execute. You can cancel a background process if you know its process ID.

kill

The **kill** command aborts a process. The command's format is:

> **kill** *PID(s)*

kill terminates the designated process IDs (shown under the PID heading in the **ps** listing). If you do not know the process ID, do a **ps** first to display the status of your processes.

In the following example, the "**sleep** *n*" command simply causes a process to "go to sleep" for *n* number of seconds. We enter two commands, **sleep** and **who**, on the same line, as a background process.

```
% (sleep 60; who)&
[1] 21087
% ps
  PID     TTY    TIME   COMMAND
 20055    4      0:10   sh
 21087    4      0:01   sh
 21088    4      0:00   sleep
 21089    4      0:02   ps
% kill 21088
Terminated
% tom       tty2    Aug 30   11:27
 grace      tty4    Aug 30   12:24
 tim        tty5    Aug 30   07:52
 dale       tty7    Aug 30   14:34
```

We decided that 60 seconds was too long a time to wait for the output of **who**. The **ps** listing showed that **sleep** had the process ID number 21088, so we used this PID to kill the **sleep** process. You should see a message like "terminated" or "killed"; if you don't, use another **ps** command to be sure the process has been killed.

The **who** command is executed immediately, since it is no longer waiting on **sleep**; it lists the users logged into the system.

Problem checklist

The process didn't die when I told it to.

Some processes can be hard to kill. If a normal kill of these processes is not working, enter "**kill** −9 *PID*". This is a sure kill and can destroy almost anything, including the shell that is interpreting it.

In addition, if you've run an interpreted program (like a shell script), you may not be able to kill all dependent processes by killing the interpreter process that got it all started; you may need to kill them individually. However, killing a process that is feeding data into a pipe will generally kill any processes receiving that data.

7

Where to Go from Here

Standard UNIX Documentation

Now that you've come to the end of this guide, you might want to know the options to the commands we've introduced and the many other UNIX commands. You're now ready to consult your system's documentation.

Different system manufacturers have adapted UNIX documentation in different ways. However, almost all UNIX documentation is derived from a manual originally called the *UNIX Programmer's Manual*. One section you'll want to consult is the one that lists general UNIX commands like **who** and **ls**. There's probably another section with tutorials and extended documentation.

Many UNIX installations (especially larger systems with plenty of disk space) have individual manual pages stored on the computer; users can read them online.

If you want to know the correct syntax for entering a command or the particular features of a program, enter the command **man** and the name of the command. The syntax is:

> **man** *command*

For example, if you want to find information about the program **mail**, which allows you to send messages to other users, you would enter:

```
% man mail
        .
        .
%
```

The output of **man** may be filtered through the **more** command automatically. If it isn't, just pipe the output of **man** to **more** (or **pg**).

After you enter the command, the screen will fill up with text. Press SPACE or RETURN to read more.

Some systems also have a command called **apropos** or **man −k** to help you locate a command if you have an idea of what it does but are not sure of its correct name. Enter **apropos** followed by a descriptive word; you'll get a list of commands that might help.

Linux systems, and many other systems, may also have a command called **info**. It serves the same purpose as **man**: to document system commands. The **info** output is in a different format, though. The syntax to start **info** is:

> info *command*

For example, if you want to find information about the program **find**, which searches for files, you would enter **info find**. After you enter the command, the screen will fill up with text. Press SPACE to read more or "q" to quit.

Shell Aliases and Functions

If you type command names that are hard for you to remember, or command lines that seem too long, you'll want to learn about *shell aliases and functions*. These shell features let you abbreviate commands, command lines, and long series of commands. In most cases, you can replace them with a single word or a word and a few arguments. For example, one of the long pipelines in Chapter 5, *Redirecting I/O*, could be replaced by an alias or function named (for instance) "aug". When you type **aug** at a shell prompt, the shell would list files modified in August, sorted by size.

Making an alias or function is almost as simple as typing in the command line or lines that you want to run. The references in Appendix A, *Reading List*, have more information. Shell aliases and functions are actually a simple case of shell programming.

Programming

Out of the hundreds of UNIX commands that have been developed, the commands for editing files are probably among the first that you should learn. As you become more familiar with other UNIX commands, you can customize your working environment and also create commands to do just what you need.

We have mentioned earlier that the shell is the system's command interpreter. It reads each command you enter at your terminal and performs the operation that you called for. The system administrator decides the type of shell that runs when you log in to your account.

The shell is just an ordinary program that can be called by a UNIX command. However, it contains some features (like variables, control structures, and so on) that make it similar to a programming language. You can save a series of shell commands in a file, called a *shell script*, to accomplish specialized functions.

Programming the shell should be attempted only when you are reasonably confident of your ability to use UNIX commands. UNIX is quite a powerful tool and its capabilities become more apparent when you try your hand at shell programming.

Take time to learn the basics. Then, when you're faced with a new task, take time to browse through references to find programs or options that will help you get the job done more easily. Once you've done that, learn how to build shell scripts so that you never have to type a complicated command sequence more than once.

You might also want to learn Perl. Like the shell, Perl interprets script files full of commands. But Perl has a steeper learning curve than the shell. Also, since you've already learned a fair amount about the shell and UNIX commands by reading this book, you're almost ready to start writing shell scripts now; on the other hand, Perl will take longer to learn. But if you have sophisticated needs, learning Perl is another way to use even more of the power of your UNIX system.

A

Reading List

This section lists a few good books in several areas.

General UNIX Books

- *Harley Hahn's Student Guide to UNIX*, second edition; McGraw-Hill; ISBN 0-07-025492-3; 1996. Not just for students, this is a complete and very readable guide to UNIX and networking.

- *UNIX for the Impatient* by Paul W. Abrahams and Bruce Larson; Addison-Wesley; 1996. Terse and detailed, for people comfortable with technical material.

- *UNIX Power Tools*, second edition, by Jerry Peek, Tim O'Reilly, Mike Loukides, and others; O'Reilly & Associates; ISBN 1-56592-260-3; 1997. A huge collection of tips, techniques, and concepts for making intermediate users into advanced users.

- *UNIX in a Nutshell: System V Edition* by Daniel Gilly and the staff of O'Reilly & Associates; ISBN 1-56592-001-5; 1992. From user commands to programmers' utilities, this book covers UNIX with concise descriptions and illustrative examples.

- *Linux in a Nutshell* by Jessica Perry Hekman and the staff of O'Reilly & Associates; ISBN 1-56592-167-4; 1997. A complete reference for Linux.

Text Processing and Programming

- *Learning the vi Editor* by Linda Lamb; O'Reilly & Associates; ISBN 0-937175-67-6; 1992. A complete introduction to vi, structured like *UNIX in a Nutshell.*

- *Learning GNU Emacs*, second edition, by Deb Cameron & Bill Rosenblatt; O'Reilly & Associates; ISBN 1-56592-152-6; 1996. Emacs doesn't come with some versions of UNIX, but users find and install it— especially the version called GNU Emacs.

- *Learning Perl*, second edition, by Randal L. Schwartz and Tom Christiansen; O'Reilly & Associates; ISBN 1-56592-284-0; 1997. An introduction to one of the most popular and powerful ways to process text and data and use all the power in your computer system.

Shells

- *UNIX Shell Programming* by Stephen G. Kochan and Patrick H. Wood; Howard Sams; ISBN 0-672-48448-X; 1990. An excellent introduction to Bourne and Korn shell programming with lots of illustrative examples.

- *Learning the Korn Shell* by Bill Rosenblatt; O'Reilly & Associates; ISBN 1-56592-054-6; 1993. A guide to using and programming the Korn shell.

- *Learning the bash Shell* by Cameron Newham and Bill Rosenblatt; O'Reilly & Associates; ISBN 1-56592-347-2; second edition to be published early 1998. Using and programming a freely available shell that's popular on Linux.

The X Window System

- *X Window System User's Guide, Volume 3, OSF/Motif edition*; Valerie Quercia and Tim O'Reilly; O'Reilly & Associates; ISBN 1-56592-015-5; 1993. A thorough guide to using and customizing the OSF/Motif graphical interface to X. Easy for beginners, but thorough enough to be a guide for experienced users.

B

Reference

Commands and Their Meanings

cancel *request*	Cancel an **lp** print request.
cat *files*	Display one or more files.
cd	Change to home directory.
cd *pathname*	Change working directory to *pathname*.
cp *old new*	Copy *old* file to *new* file.
date	Display current date and time.
grep *"pattern" files*	Show lines matching *pattern* in *files*.
kill *PID*	End process *PID*.
lp *files*	Send *files* to default printer.
lpq	Check requests on **lpr** printer queue.
lpr *files*	Send *files* to default printer.
lprm *request*	Cancel an **lpr** print request.
lpstat	Check requests on **lp** printer queue.
ls	List names of files in working directory.
mail	Read your own mail.
mail *user*	Send mail to *user*.
man *command*	Display manual page of *command*.
mkdir *pathname*	Create a new directory with *pathname*.
more *files*	Display one screenful of each *file* at a time.
mv *old new*	Move or rename *old* file to *new* file.
pg *files*	Display one screenful of each *file* at a time.
ps	List your processes and their PIDs.
pwd	Print working (current) directory name.
rm *files*	Remove *files*.

rmdir *pathname*   Remove empty directory with *pathname*.
sort *files*   Sort lines of *files*.
who   List users currently on system.
who am i   Display listing for this session.

Special Symbols

| Set up a pipe.
>   Redirect output to a file.
<   Redirect input from a file.
>>   Append output to an existing file.
/   Separator used in pathnames.
.   Current directory.
..   Parent directory.
&   Process command in the background.
*   Match any number of characters in filename.
?   Match any single character in filename.
[ ]   Match any one of the enclosed characters in filename.
;   Command separator.
( )   Group commands.

Index

Symbols

& for background processes, 75
* wildcard, 51-52, 59
[ ] as wildcards, 52
. (dot)
    . directory shortcut, 35, 54
    .. directory shortcut, 32, 35, 54
    in filenames, 51
> (output redirection operator), 67-70
>> (output redirection operator), 70
- (hyphen) for command options, 9
< (input redirection operator), 67
| for I/O redirection, 67
? wildcard, 51
; (semicolon) on command line, 10
/ (slash)
    in pathnames, 30-32
    for root directory, 29, 31

A

absolute pathnames, 30-31
access modes, 37
access permissions (see permissions)
account, customizing, 47-49
aliases, shell, 81
ampersand (&) for background pro-
      cesses, 75
appending text to files, 70
apropos command, 81
arguments, command, 9

Symbols

ascii command (ftp), 56
asterisk (*) as wildcard, 51-52, 59

B

background processing, 75-79
    cancelling processes, 78-79
    checking on processes, 76-77
BACKSPACE key, 7, 48
bg command, 76
binary command (ftp), 56
block cursor, 21
brackets [ ] as wildcards, 52

C

calculator program (on X), 19
cancel command, 64
cancelling
    background processes, 78-79
    print jobs, 64
cat command, 39, 68-69
cd command, 33, 56
chattr command (Linux), 42
chmod command, 37, 41-42
clicking the mouse, 21
clobbering files, 69
Close menu item (mwm), 24
command line, 6-8
    correcting mistakes on, 7-8

About the Author

Jerry Peek has used UNIX since the early 1980s. He has consulted on UNIX and VMS, developed and taught UNIX courses, been a staff writer for O'Reilly & Associates, and worked as a programmer and system administrator. He's now doing graduate studies in Computer Science. When Jerry gets a minute or a month, he hikes and bicycles the California coast and travels to obscure places in Latin America.

Grace Todino is currently residing in Oman. While working as a technical writer at O'Reilly & Associates, Inc., Grace was one of the original authors of the Nutshell Handbooks, *Managing UUCP and Usenet* and *Using UUCP and Usenet.*

John Strang now finds himself "a consumer—rather than a producer—of Nutshells." He is currently a diagnostic radiologist (MD) at Stanford University. He is married to a pediatrician, Susie, and they have two children, Katie and Alex. John enjoys hiking, bicycling, and dabbling in other sciences. He plans to use his experience as an author at ORA to write his own book on radiology.

Colophon

Our look is the result of reader comments, our own experimentation, and distribution channels.

Distinctive covers complement our distinctive approach to technical topics, breathing personality and life into potentially dry subjects. UNIX and its attendant programs can be unruly beasts. Nutshell Handbooks help you tame them.

The animal featured on the cover of *Learning the UNIX Operating System* is the horned owl. The horned owl is the most powerful of the North American owls, measuring from 18 to 25 inches long. This nocturnal bird of prey feeds exclusively on animals—primarily rabbits, rodents, and birds, including other owls—which it locates by sound rather than sight, its night vision being little better than ours. To aid in its hunting, an owl has very soft feathers which muffle the sound of its motion, making it virtually silent in flight. A tree-dwelling bird, it generally chooses to inhabit the old nests of other large birds such as hawks and crows rather than build its own nest.

Edie Freedman designed this cover and the entire UNIX bestiary that appears on other Nutshell Handbooks. The beasts themselves are adapted from 19th-century engravings from the Dover Pictorial Archive.

The inside layout was designed by Nancy Priest and implemented in troff by Lenny Muellner. The text of this book is set in ITC Garamond Light and Garamond Book. The text pages are formatted in troff. Figures were created by Chris Reilley and updated by Robert Romano in Macromedia Freehand. The cover was produced in QuarkXPress.

Whenever possible, our books use RepKover™, a durable and flexible lay-flat binding. If the page count exceeds RepKover's limit, perfect binding is used.

More Titles from O'Reilly

Unix Basics

Learning GNU Emacs, 2nd Edition

By Debra Cameron, Bill Rosenblatt &
Eric Raymond
2nd Edition September 1996
560 pages, ISBN 1-56592-152-6

Learning GNU Emacs is an introduction to Version 19.30 of the GNU
Emacs editor, one of the most widely
used and powerful editors available
under UNIX. It provides a solid introduction to basic editing, a look at several important "editing
modes" (special Emacs features for editing specific types of
documents, including email, Usenet News, and the World
Wide Web), and a brief introduction to customization and
Emacs LISP programming. The book is aimed at new Emacs
users, whether or not they are programmers. Includes quick-
reference card.

Learning the bash Shell, 2nd Edition

By Cameron Newham &
Bill Rosenblatt
2nd Edition January 1998
336 pages, ISBN 1-56592-347-2

This second edition covers all of the
features of bash Version 2.0, while
still applying to bash Version 1.x. It
includes one-dimensional arrays,
parameter expansion, more pattern-
matching operations, new commands, security improvements,
additions to ReadLine, improved configuration and installation,
and an additional programming aid, the bash shell debugger.

sed & awk, 2nd Edition

By Dale Dougherty & Arnold Robbins
2nd Edition March 1997
432 pages, ISBN 1-56592-225-5

sed & awk describes two text manipulation
programs that are mainstays of the UNIX
programmer's toolbox. This new edition
covers the sed and awk programs as they
are now mandated by the POSIX standard
and includes discussion of the GNU versions of these programs.

Learning the Korn Shell

By Bill Rosenblatt
1st Edition June 1993
360 pages, ISBN 1-56592-054-6

This Nutshell Handbook is a thorough
introduction to the Korn shell, both as
a user interface and as a programming
language. The Korn shell is a program
that interprets UNIX commands. It has
many features that aren't found in other
shells, including command history. This book provides a
clear and concise explanation of the Korn shell's features.
It explains ksh string operations, co-processes, signals and
signal handling, and command-line interpretation. The book
also includes real-life programming examples and a Korn
shell debugger called kshdb, the only known implementation
of a shell debugger anywhere.

Using csh and tcsh

By Paul DuBois
1st Edition August 1995
242 pages, ISBN 1-56592-132-1

Using csh and tcsh describes from the
beginning how to use these shells
interactively to get your work done
faster with less typing. You'll learn
how to make your prompt tell you
where you are (no more pwd); use
what you've typed before (history); type long command lines
with few keystrokes (command and filename completion);
remind yourself of filenames when in the middle of typing a
command; and edit a botched command without retyping it.

Learning the vi Editor, 5th Edition

By Linda Lamb
5th Edition October 1990
192 pages, ISBN 0-937175-67-6

This book is a complete guide to text
editing with vi, the editor available on
nearly every UNIX system. Early chapters
cover the basics; later chapters explain
more advanced editing tools, such as ex
commands and global search and
replacement.

O'REILLY™

Unix Basics

SCO UNIX in a Nutshell

By Ellie Cutler &
the staff of O'Reilly & Associates
1st Edition February 1994
590 pages, ISBN 1-56592-037-6

The desktop reference to SCO UNIX and Open Desktop®, this version of *UNIX in a Nutshell* shows you what's under the hood of your SCO system. It isn't a scaled-down quick reference of common commands, but a complete reference containing all user, programming, administration, and networking commands.

UNIX in a Nutshell: System V Edition

By Daniel Gilly &
the staff of O'Reilly & Associates
2nd Edition June 1992
444 pages, ISBN 1-56592-001-5

You may have seen UNIX quick-reference guides, but you've never seen anything like *UNIX in a Nutshell*. Not a scaled-down quick reference of common commands, *UNIX in a Nutshell* is a complete reference containing all commands and options, along with generous descriptions and examples that put the commands in context. For all but the thorniest UNIX problems, this one reference should be all the documentation you need. Covers System V, Releases 3 and 4, and Solaris 2.0.

What You Need to Know: When You Can't Find Your UNIX System Administrator

By Linda Mui
1st Edition April 1995
156 pages, ISBN 1-56592-104-6

This book is written for UNIX users, who are often cast adrift in a confusing environment. It provides the background and practical solutions you need to solve problems you're likely to encounter—problems with logging in, printing, sharing files, running programs, managing space resources, etc. It also describes the kind of info to gather when you're asking for a diagnosis from a busy sys admin. And, it gives you a list of site-specific information that you should know, as well as a place to write it down.

Volume 3M: X Window System User's Guide, Motif Edition, 2nd Edition

By Valerie Quercia & Tim O'Reilly
2nd Edition January 1993
956 pages, ISBN 1-56592-015-5

The *X Window System User's Guide, Motif Edition* orients the new user to window system concepts and provides detailed tutorials for many client programs, including the xtermterminal emulator and the twm, uwm, and mwmwindow managers. Later chapters explain how to customize the X environment. Revised for Motif 1.2 and X11 Release 5.

O'REILLY™

TO ORDER: **800-998-9938** • *order@oreilly.com* • *http://www.oreilly.com/*
OUR PRODUCTS ARE AVAILABLE AT A BOOKSTORE OR SOFTWARE STORE NEAR YOU.
FOR INFORMATION: **800-998-9938** • **707-829-0515** • *info@oreilly.com*

How to stay in touch with O'Reilly

1. Visit Our Award-Winning Site

http://www.oreilly.com/

★ "Top 100 Sites on the Web" —*PC Magazine*
★ "Top 5% Web sites" —*Point Communications*
★ "3-Star site" —*The McKinley Group*

Our web site contains a library of comprehensive product information (including book excerpts and tables of contents), downloadable software, background articles, interviews with technology leaders, links to relevant sites, book cover art, and more. File us in your Bookmarks or Hotlist!

2. Join Our Email Mailing Lists

New Product Releases

To receive automatic email with brief descriptions of all new O'Reilly products as they are released, send email to:
listproc@online.oreilly.com
Put the following information in the first line of your message (*not* in the Subject field):
subscribe oreilly-news

O'Reilly Events

If you'd also like us to send information about trade show events, special promotions, and other O'Reilly events, send email to:
listproc@online.oreilly.com
Put the following information in the first line of your message (*not* in the Subject field):
subscribe oreilly-events

3. Get Examples from Our Books via FTP

There are two ways to access an archive of example files from our books:

Regular FTP

* ftp to:
  ftp.oreilly.com
  (login: anonymous
  password: your email address)
* Point your web browser to:
  ftp://ftp.oreilly.com/

FTPMAIL

* Send an email message to:
  ftpmail@online.oreilly.com
  (Write "help" in the message body)

4. Contact Us via Email

order@oreilly.com
To place a book or software order online. Good for North American and international customers.

subscriptions@oreilly.com
To place an order for any of our newsletters or periodicals.

books@oreilly.com
General questions about any of our books.

software@oreilly.com
For general questions and product information about our software. Check out O'Reilly Software Online at **http://software.oreilly.com/** for software and technical support information. Registered O'Reilly software users send your questions to:
website-support@oreilly.com

cs@oreilly.com
For answers to problems regarding your order or our products.

booktech@oreilly.com
For book content technical questions or corrections.

proposals@oreilly.com
To submit new book or software proposals to our editors and product managers.

international@oreilly.com
For information about our international distributors or translation queries. For a list of our distributors outside of North America check out:
http://www.oreilly.com/www/order/country.html

O'Reilly & Associates, Inc.
101 Morris Street, Sebastopol, CA 95472 USA
TEL   707-829-0515 or 800-998-9938
      (6am to 5pm PST)
FAX   707-829-0104

Titles from O'Reilly

International Distributors

UK, EUROPE, MIDDLE EAST AND NORTHERN AFRICA (except France, Germany, Switzerland, & Austria)

INQUIRIES
International Thomson Publishing Europe
Berkshire House
168-173 High Holborn
London WC1V 7AA, UK
Telephone: 44-171-497-1422
Fax: 44-171-497-1426
Email: itpint@itps.co.uk

ORDERS
International Thomson Publishing Services, Ltd.
Cheriton House, North Way
Andover, Hampshire SP10 5BE,
United Kingdom
Telephone: 44-264-342-832 (UK)
Telephone: 44-264-342-806 (outside UK)
Fax: 44-264-364418 (UK)
Fax: 44-264-342761 (outside UK)
UK & Eire orders: itpuk@itps.co.uk
International orders: itpint@itps.co.uk

FRANCE
Editions Eyrolles
61 bd Saint-Germain
75240 Paris Cedex 05
France
Fax: 33-01-44-41-11-44

FRENCH LANGUAGE BOOKS
All countries except Canada
Telephone: 33-01-44-41-46-16
Email: geodif@eyrolles.com

ENGLISH LANGUAGE BOOKS
Telephone: 33-01-44-41-11-87
Email: distribution@eyrolles.com

GERMANY, SWITZERLAND, AND AUSTRIA

INQUIRIES
O'Reilly Verlag
Balthasarstr. 81
D-50670 Köln
Germany
Telephone: 49-221-97-31-60-0
Fax: 49-221-97-31-60-8
Email: anfragen@oreilly.de

ORDERS
International Thomson Publishing
Königswinterer Straße 418
53227 Bonn, Germany
Telephone: 49-228-97024 0
Fax: 49-228-441342
Email: order@oreilly.de

JAPAN
O'Reilly Japan, Inc.
Kiyoshige Building 2F
12-Banchi, Sanei-cho
Shinjuku-ku
Tokyo 160 Japan
Tel: 81-3-3356-5227
Fax: 81-3-3356-5261
Email: kenji@oreilly.com

INDIA
Computer Bookshop (India) PVT. Ltd.
190 Dr. D.N. Road, Fort
Bombay 400 001 India
Tel: 91-22-207-0989
Fax: 91-22-262-3551
Email: cbsbom@giasbm01.vsnl.net.in

HONG KONG
City Discount Subscription Service Ltd.
Unit D, 3rd Floor, Yan's Tower
27 Wong Chuk Hang Road
Aberdeen, Hong Kong
Telephone: 852-2580-3539
Fax: 852-2580-6463
Email: citydis@ppn.com.hk

KOREA
Hanbit Publishing, Inc.
Sonyoung Bldg. 202
Yeksam-dong 736-36
Kangnam-ku
Seoul, Korea
Telephone: 822-554-9610
Fax: 822-556-0363
Email: hant93@chollian.dacom.co.kr

TAIWAN
ImageArt Publishing, Inc.
4/fl. No. 65 Shinyi Road Sec. 4
Taipei, Taiwan, R.O.C.
Telephone: 886-2708-5770
Fax: 886-2705-6690
Email: marie@ms1.hinet.net

SINGAPORE, MALAYSIA, AND THAILAND
Longman Singapore
25 First Lok Yan Road
Singapore 2262
Telephone: 65-268-2666
Fax: 65-268-7023
Email: daniel@longman.com.sg

PHILIPPINES
Mutual Books, Inc.
429-D Shaw Boulevard
Mandaluyong City, Metro
Manila, Philippines
Telephone: 632-725-7538
Fax: 632-721-3056
Email: mbikikog@mnl.sequel.net

CHINA
Ron's DataCom Co., Ltd.
79 Dongwu Avenue
Dongxihu District
Wuhan 430040
China
Telephone: 86-27-83892568
Fax: 86-27-83222108
Email: hongfeng@public.wh.hb.cn

AUSTRALIA
WoodsLane Pty. Ltd.
7/5 Vuko Place, Warriewood NSW 2102
P.O. Box 935,
Mona Vale NSW 2103
Australia
Telephone: 61-2-9970-5111
Fax: 61-2-9970-5002
Email: info@woodslane.com.au

ALL OTHER ASIA COUNTRIES
O'Reilly & Associates, Inc.
101 Morris Street
Sebastopol, CA 95472 USA
Telephone: 707-829-0515
Fax: 707-829-0104
Email: order@oreilly.com

THE AMERICAS
McGraw-Hill Interamericana Editores,
S.A. de C.V.
Cedro No. 512
Col. Atlampa 06450
Mexico, D.F.
Telephone: 52-5-541-3155
Fax: 52-5-541-4913
Email: mcgraw-hill@infosel.net.mx

SOUTHERN AFRICA
International Thomson Publishing Southern Africa
Building 18, Constantia Park
138 Sixteenth Road
P.O. Box 2459
Halfway House, 1685 South Africa
Tel: 27-11-805-4819
Fax: 27-11-805-3648

O'REILLY™

TO ORDER: **800-998-9938** • **order@oreilly.com** • **http://www.oreilly.com/**
OUR PRODUCTS ARE AVAILABLE AT A BOOKSTORE OR SOFTWARE STORE NEAR YOU.
FOR INFORMATION: **800-998-9938** • **707-829-0515** • **info@oreilly.com**